chocolate

THE AUSTRALIAN
Women's Weekly

I can't think of anything that excites the tastebuds as much as chocolate does. And deliberating over which recipes to include in this book was as maddening as selecting truffles for a gift box (you know, hard work but someone's got to...). But I feel sure you'll approve: not only is every recipe a delicious individual in its own right, there isn't one that's hard to make – the hard bit will be choosing which one!

Pamela Clark

Food Director

contents

cakes   4

biscuits and slices   48

pastries and tarts   66

desserts   82

after-dinner treats   110

glossary   115

index   117

conversion chart   119

white chocolate mud cake

preparation time 50 minutes (plus cooling time) **cooking time** 1 hour 45 minutes **serves** 12

250g butter, chopped

180g white eating chocolate, chopped coarsely

1½ cups (330g) caster sugar

¾ cup (180ml) milk

1½ cups (225g) plain flour

½ cup (75g) self-raising flour

½ teaspoon vanilla extract

2 eggs, beaten lightly

WHITE CHOCOLATE GANACHE

½ cup (125ml) thickened cream

360g white eating chocolate, chopped finely

1 Preheat oven to moderately slow. Grease deep 20cm-round cake pan; line base and side with baking paper.
2 Combine butter, chocolate, sugar and milk in medium saucepan; stir over low heat until melted. Transfer mixture to large bowl; cool 15 minutes.
3 Stir in sifted flours, extract and egg; pour into prepared pan. Bake, uncovered, in moderately slow oven about 1 hour 40 minutes; cool cake in pan.
4 Meanwhile, make white chocolate ganache.
5 Turn cake onto serving plate top-side up. Spread ganache all over cake; top with chocolate curls, if desired.
WHITE CHOCOLATE GANACHE Bring cream to a boil in small saucepan; pour over chocolate in medium heatproof bowl, stir with wooden spoon until chocolate melts. Cover bowl; refrigerate, stirring occasionally, about 30 minutes or until ganache is of a spreadable consistency.

cakes

family chocolate cake

preparation time 20 minutes (plus cooling time) **cooking time** 1 hour **serves** 20

2 cups (500ml) water

3 cups (660g) caster sugar

250g butter, chopped

⅓ cup (35g) cocoa powder

1 teaspoon bicarbonate of soda

3 cups (450g) self-raising flour

4 eggs, beaten lightly

FUDGE FROSTING

90g butter

⅓ cup (80ml) water

½ cup (110g) caster sugar

1½ cups (240g) icing sugar

⅓ cup (35g) cocoa powder

1 Preheat oven to moderate. Grease deep 26.5cm x 33cm (14 cup/3.5 litre) baking dish; line base with baking paper.

2 Combine the water, sugar, butter and combined sifted cocoa powder and soda in medium saucepan; stir over heat, without boiling, until sugar dissolves. Bring to a boil, then reduce heat; simmer, uncovered, 5 minutes. Transfer mixture to large bowl; cool to room temperature.

3 Add flour and egg to bowl; beat with electric mixer until mixture is smooth and paler in colour. Pour mixture into prepared dish.

4 Bake cake in moderate oven about 50 minutes. Stand cake in baking dish 10 minutes before turning onto wire rack; turn cake top-side up to cool. Spread cold cake with fudge frosting.

FUDGE FROSTING Combine butter, the water and caster sugar in small saucepan; stir over heat, without boiling, until sugar dissolves. Sift icing sugar and cocoa powder into small bowl, then gradually stir in hot butter mixture. Cover; refrigerate about 20 minutes or until frosting thickens. Beat with wooden spoon until spreadable.

tips Choose a perfectly level-bottomed baking dish; one made from cast aluminium is the best choice, but almost any type will work.
If the cake appears to be cooking too quickly in the corners of the dish, reduce oven temperature to moderately slow; this will increase cooking time by up to 15 minutes.

cakes

mocha syrup cake

preparation time 10 minutes **cooking time** 45 minutes **serves** 8

3 teaspoons instant coffee powder

1 tablespoon hot water

3 eggs

¾ cup (165g) caster sugar

1 cup (150g) self-raising flour

1 tablespoon cocoa powder

150g butter, melted

COFFEE SYRUP

¾ cup (165g) caster sugar

¾ cup (180ml) water

3 teaspoons instant coffee powder

1 Preheat oven to moderate. Grease 21cm baba cake pan.

2 Combine coffee and the water; stir until dissolved.

3 Beat eggs in bowl with electric mixer about 8 minutes or until thick and creamy. Gradually add sugar; beat until dissolved between each addition.

4 Transfer to large bowl, fold in sifted flour and cocoa powder, then butter and coffee mixture. Pour mixture into prepared pan.

5 Bake in moderate oven about 40 minutes. Stand cake in pan 5 minutes before turning onto baking-paper-covered wire rack, stand rack over a tray.

6 Reserve ¼ cup of the hot coffee syrup. Pour remaining syrup over hot cake. Serve drizzled with reserved syrup.

COFFEE SYRUP Combine ingredients in small saucepan; stir over heat, without boiling, until sugar is dissolved. Bring to a boil, remove from heat; transfer syrup to heatproof jug.

tip This cake can be made a day ahead; store in an airtight container.

chocolate buttermilk cake

preparation time 20 minutes (plus cooling and chilling time) **cooking time** 1 hour **serves** 8 to 10

180g butter, chopped

1 teaspoon vanilla extract

1½ cups (330g) caster sugar

4 eggs, separated

¾ cup (110g) self-raising flour

⅓ cup (35g) cocoa powder

¾ cup (180ml) buttermilk

CHOCOLATE FILLING

400g dark eating chocolate, melted

250g butter, melted

½ cup (80g) icing sugar

1 Preheat oven to moderate. Grease deep 20cm-round cake pan; line base with baking paper.

2 Beat butter, extract and sugar in small bowl with electric mixer until light and fluffy; beat in egg yolks, one at a time, until just combined. Transfer mixture to large bowl; stir in sifted dry ingredients and buttermilk.

3 Beat egg whites in clean small bowl with electric mixer until soft peaks form; fold into cake mixture in two batches. Pour cake mixture into prepared pan. Bake in moderate oven about 1 hour. Cool cake in pan.

4 Make chocolate filling; reserve about 1 cup. Split cake into three layers. Place one layer on serving plate, spread thinly with some of the remaining chocolate filling; repeat layering with remaining cake layers and filling. Spread reserved filling all over cake. Refrigerate 3 hours before serving.

CHOCOLATE FILLING Combine chocolate and butter in medium bowl; stir in sifted icing sugar. Cool filling to room temperature; beat with wooden spoon until thick and spreadable.

tips Cake can be made a day ahead and kept, covered, in the refrigerator. The butter and chocolate are suitable to microwave.

cakes

sticky chocolate date cake

preparation time 15 minutes (plus standing time) **cooking time** 1 hour **serves** 8 to 10

1⅓ cups (200g) seeded dried dates, chopped

1¾ cups (430ml) water

1 teaspoon bicarbonate of soda

80g butter, chopped

⅔ cup (150g) caster sugar

2 eggs

1 cup (150g) self-raising flour

⅓ cup (35g) cocoa powder

⅔ cup (70g) toasted pecans, chopped

BUTTERSCOTCH SAUCE

1¼ cups (280g) firmly packed brown sugar

80g butter

300ml cream

1 Preheat oven to moderate. Grease deep 22cm-round cake pan; line base with baking paper.

2 Combine dates and the water in small saucepan; bring to a boil. Remove from heat, add soda; cover, stand 5 minutes. Blend or process until smooth.

3 Beat butter and sugar in small bowl with electric mixer until combined; beat in eggs quickly, one at a time (mixture will curdle at this stage). Transfer mixture to large bowl; fold in sifted flour and cocoa powder, then add nuts and warm date mixture, in two batches. Pour mixture into prepared pan.

4 Bake in moderate oven about 1 hour. Stand cake in pan 10 minutes before turning onto serving plate.

5 Serve pudding with hot butterscotch sauce and whipped cream, if desired.
   BUTTERSCOTCH SAUCE Combine ingredients in saucepan; stir over heat, without boiling, until sugar is dissolved. Simmer, without stirring, 3 minutes.

cakes

12

mississippi mud cake

preparation time 25 minutes (plus cooling time) **cooking time** 1 hour 35 minutes **serves** 10

This popular cake is a delectable alternative to fruit cake for weddings and other occasions. It is also wonderful after dinner with coffee, served warm or at room temperature with double cream.

250g butter, chopped

150g dark eating chocolate, chopped

2 cups (440g) caster sugar

1 cup (250ml) hot water

⅓ cup (80ml) coffee-flavoured liqueur

1 tablespoon instant coffee powder

1½ cups (225g) plain flour

¼ cup (35g) self-raising flour

¼ cup (25g) cocoa powder

2 eggs, beaten lightly

1   Preheat oven to moderately slow. Grease deep 20cm-round cake pan; line base and side with baking paper.

2   Combine butter, chocolate, sugar, the water, liqueur and coffee powder in medium saucepan. Using wooden spoon, stir over low heat until chocolate melts.

3   Transfer mixture to large bowl; cool 15 minutes. Whisk in combined sifted flours and cocoa powder, then egg. Pour mixture into prepared pan.

4   Bake in moderately slow oven about 1½ hours. Stand cake in pan 30 minutes before turning onto wire rack; turn cake top-side up to cool.

tips Cover the cake loosely with foil about halfway through the baking time if it starts to overbrown.
The cake will keep for up to one week in an airtight container in refrigerator.

chocolate roulade with coffee cream

preparation time 20 minutes (plus cooling and chilling time) **cooking time** 10 minutes **serves** 8

1 tablespoon caster sugar

200g dark cooking chocolate, chopped coarsely

¼ cup (60ml) hot water

1 tablespoon instant coffee powder

4 eggs, separated

½ cup (110g) caster sugar, extra

1 teaspoon hot water, extra

300ml whipping cream

2 tablespoons coffee-flavoured liqueur

1 tablespoon icing sugar

1 Preheat oven to moderate. Grease 25cm x 30cm swiss roll pan; line base with baking paper. Place a piece of baking paper cut the same size as swiss roll pan on board or bench; sprinkle evenly with caster sugar.

2 Combine chocolate, the water and half of the coffee powder in large heatproof bowl. Stir over large saucepan of simmering water until smooth; remove from heat.

3 Beat egg yolks and extra caster sugar in small bowl with electric mixer until thick and creamy; fold egg mixture into warm chocolate mixture.

4 Meanwhile, beat egg whites in clean small bowl with electric mixer until soft peaks form; fold egg whites, in two batches, into chocolate mixture. Spread into prepared pan; bake in moderate oven about 10 minutes.

5 Turn cake onto sugared paper, peel baking paper away; use serrated knife to cut away crisp edges from all sides. Cover cake with tea towel; cool.

6 Dissolve remaining coffee powder in the extra water in small bowl. Add cream, liqueur and icing sugar; beat with electric mixer until firm peaks form. Spread cake evenly with cream mixture. Roll cake, from long side, by lifting paper and using it to guide the roll into shape. Cover roll; refrigerate 30 minutes before serving.

tip Be sure you beat the egg yolk mixture until thick, and the egg whites only until soft peaks form. Overbeating will dry out the egg whites and make them difficult to fold into the chocolate mixture.

cakes

upside-down chocolate caramel nut cake

preparation time 15 minutes **cooking time** 1 hour 20 minutes **serves** 10

2 tablespoons chopped, toasted macadamias

2 tablespoons chopped, toasted pistachios

2 tablespoons chopped, toasted walnuts

125g butter, chopped

1 cup (220g) firmly packed brown sugar

3 eggs

1 cup (150g) self-raising flour

¼ cup (35g) plain flour

¼ teaspoon bicarbonate of soda

⅓ cup (35g) cocoa powder

100g dark eating chocolate, melted

¾ cup (180ml) milk

CARAMEL TOPPING

40g butter

¼ cup (55g) firmly packed brown sugar

2 tablespoons cream

1   Preheat oven to moderately slow. Grease deep 20cm-round cake pan; line base with baking paper.

2   Make caramel topping. Pour hot topping over base of prepared pan, sprinkle combined nuts over caramel; freeze while preparing cake mixture.

3   Beat butter and sugar in small bowl with electric mixer until light and fluffy. Beat in eggs, one at a time, until just combined between each addition.

4   Stir in sifted flours, soda and cocoa powder, then chocolate and milk. Spread cake mixture over caramel nut topping.

5   Bake in moderately slow oven about 1 hour 10 minutes. Stand cake in pan 15 minutes before turning onto wire rack to cool.
    CARAMEL TOPPING Combine butter, sugar and cream in small saucepan; stir over low heat, without boiling, until sugar is dissolved. Bring to a boil, then remove from heat.

tips This cake can be made a day ahead and kept in an airtight container. Use unsalted nuts.

cakes

19

low-fat chocolate fudge cake

preparation time 20 minutes **cooking time** 40 minutes **serves** 8

85g dark eating chocolate, chopped finely

½ cup (50g) cocoa powder

1 cup (200g) firmly packed brown sugar

½ cup (125ml) boiling water

2 egg yolks

¼ cup (30g) almond meal

⅓ cup (50g) wholemeal plain flour

4 egg whites

1   Preheat oven to moderate. Line base and side of deep 20cm-round cake pan with baking paper.

2   Combine chocolate, cocoa and sugar with the water in large bowl; stir until smooth. Add egg yolks; whisk to combine. Fold in almond meal and flour.

3   Beat egg whites in small bowl with electric mixer until firm peaks form. Gently fold egg white mixture into chocolate mixture, in two batches; pour into prepared pan.

4   Bake in moderate oven about 40 minutes. Stand in pan 5 minutes, then turn onto wire rack; remove paper.

tip Serve warm, dusted with icing sugar and topped with strawberries.

dark chocolate and almond torte

preparation time 20 minutes (plus standing time) **cooking time** 55 minutes **serves** 14

Candied (vienna) almonds are whole almonds coated in toffee. They are available from selected supermarkets, nut shops and gourmet food and specialty confectionery stores.

160g dark eating chocolate, chopped coarsely

160g unsalted butter, chopped

5 eggs, separated

¾ cup (165g) caster sugar

1 cup (125g) almond meal

⅔ cup (50g) toasted flaked almonds, chopped coarsely

⅓ cup (35g) coarsely grated dark eating chocolate

1 cup (140g) candied (vienna) almonds

DARK CHOCOLATE GANACHE

125g dark eating chocolate, chopped coarsely

⅓ cup (80ml) thickened cream

1 Preheat oven to moderate. Grease deep 22cm-round cake pan; line the base and side with two layers of baking paper.

2 Stir chopped chocolate and butter in small saucepan over low heat until smooth; cool to room temperature.

3 Beat egg yolks and sugar in small bowl with electric mixer until thick and creamy. Transfer to large bowl; fold in chocolate mixture, almond meal, flaked almonds and grated chocolate.

4 Beat egg whites in small bowl with electric mixer until soft peaks form; fold into chocolate mixture, in two batches. Pour mixture into prepared pan; bake, uncovered, in moderate oven about 45 minutes. Stand cake in pan 15 minutes; turn cake, top-side up, onto wire rack to cool.

5 Meanwhile, make dark chocolate ganache.

6 Spread ganache over top of cake, decorate cake with candied almonds; stand 30 minutes before serving.
DARK CHOCOLATE GANACHE Stir chocolate and cream in small saucepan over low heat until smooth.

sacher torte

preparation time 30 minutes (plus standing and cooling time) **cooking time** 30 minutes **serves** 10 to 12

150g dark eating chocolate, chopped

1 tablespoon warm water

150g butter, chopped

½ cup (110g) caster sugar

3 eggs, separated

1 cup (150g) plain flour

2 tablespoons caster sugar, extra

⅔ cup (220g) apricot jam

CHOCOLATE ICING

125g dark eating chocolate, chopped

125g butter

1 Preheat oven to moderate. Grease deep 22cm-round cake pan; line base with baking paper.

2 Melt chocolate in heatproof bowl over hot water, stir in the water; cool to room temperature.

3 Beat butter and sugar in small bowl with electric mixer until pale in colour. Beat in egg yolks one at a time, until combined between each addition. Transfer mixture to large bowl; stir in chocolate mixture, then sifted flour.

4 Beat egg whites in clean small bowl until soft peaks form, gradually add extra sugar, beat until dissolved between each addition; fold lightly into chocolate mixture. Spread mixture into prepared pan.

5 Bake in moderate oven about 30 minutes. Stand cake in pan 5 minutes before turning onto wire rack to cool; leave cake upside down to cool.

6 Split cake in half, place one half on serving plate. Heat and strain jam, brush over half of the cake. Top with remaining half of cake, brush cake all over with remaining jam. Stand about 1 hour at room temperature to allow jam to set. Make chocolate icing.

7 Spread top and side of cake with chocolate icing; set at room temperature. **CHOCOLATE ICING** Melt chocolate and butter in medium bowl over hot water, stir until smooth. Cool to room temperature until spreadable, stir occasionally; this can take up to 2 hours.

tip This icing is also suitable for piping.

double-decker mud cake

preparation time 30 minutes (plus cooling time) **cooking time** 1 hour **serves** 10

250g butter, chopped

150g white cooking chocolate, chopped coarsely

2 cups (440g) caster sugar

1 cup (250ml) milk

1½ cups (225g) plain flour

½ cup (75g) self-raising flour

1 teaspoon vanilla essence

2 eggs, beaten lightly

2 tablespoons cocoa powder

600g milk cooking chocolate, chopped coarsely

1 cup (250ml) cream

1 Preheat oven to slow. Grease two deep 20cm-round cake pans; line bases and sides with baking paper.

2 Combine butter, white chocolate, sugar and milk in medium saucepan; stir over heat, without boiling, until smooth. Transfer mixture to large bowl; cool 15 minutes.

3 Whisk sifted flours into white chocolate mixture, then whisk in essence and egg; pour half of the mixture into one of the prepared pans. Whisk sifted cocoa into remaining mixture; pour into other prepared pan. Bake cakes in slow oven about 50 minutes. Stand cakes in pans 5 minutes; turn cakes, top-side up, onto wire rack to cool.

4 Meanwhile, combine milk chocolate and cream in medium saucepan; stir over low heat until smooth. Transfer to medium bowl. Cover; refrigerate, stirring occasionally, until chocolate mixture is of spreadable consistency. Reserve 1 cup of chocolate mixture for spreading over cake.

5 Split each cooled cake in half. Centre one layer of cake on serving plate; spread with ½ cup of the remaining milk chocolate mixture. Repeat layering, alternating colours. Cover top and sides of cake with reserved milk chocolate mixture.

tip You can also melt the milk chocolate and cream in a microwave oven; cook on high (100%) about 1½ minutes, pausing to stir every 30 seconds.

cakes

gluten-free chocolate cake

preparation time 20 minutes (plus cooling time) **cooking time** 30 minutes **serves** 8

You will need one large (230g) overripe banana for this recipe. Cornflour comes in two types, wheaten and corn. Make sure you use 100% corn (maize) cornflour in this recipe.

1 cup (125g) soy flour

¾ cup (110g) maize cornflour

1¼ teaspoons bicarbonate of soda

½ cup (50g) cocoa powder

1¼ cups (275g) caster sugar

150g butter, melted

1 tablespoon white vinegar

1 cup (250ml) evaporated milk

2 eggs

½ cup mashed banana

2 tablespoons raspberry jam

300ml whipping cream

1   Preheat oven to moderate. Grease two 22cm-round sandwich cake pans; line bases with baking paper.

2   Sift flours, soda, cocoa and sugar into large bowl; add butter, vinegar and milk. Beat with electric mixer on low speed 1 minute; add eggs, banana and jam, beat on medium speed 2 minutes. Pour mixture into prepared pans.

3   Bake in moderate oven about 30 minutes. Stand cakes in pans 5 minutes before turning onto wire racks to cool.

4   Beat cream in small bowl with electric mixer until firm peaks form. Sandwich cakes with whipped cream; lightly dust with sifted icing sugar or sifted cocoa, if desired.

tips Store unfilled cakes in airtight containers for up to two days. Sandwich cake with whipped cream close to serving.
Cake not suitable to freeze.

cakes

irish cream and dark chocolate mousse cake

preparation time 30 minutes (plus cooling and refrigeration time) **cooking time** 15 minutes **serves** 12

6 eggs, separated

½ cup (80g) icing sugar

¼ cup (25g) cocoa powder

2 tablespoons cornflour

150g dark eating chocolate, melted

1 tablespoon water

600ml cream

450g dark eating chocolate, chopped coarsely, extra

¾ cup (180ml) irish cream liqueur

1 tablespoon cocoa powder, extra

1 Preheat oven to moderate. Grease 25cm x 30cm swiss roll pan; line base and sides with baking paper.

2 Beat egg yolks and icing sugar in small bowl with electric mixer until thick and creamy; transfer to large bowl. Fold in combined sifted cocoa and cornflour, then chocolate; fold in the water.

3 Beat egg whites in medium bowl with electric mixer until soft peaks form. Fold egg whites, in two batches, into chocolate mixture. Spread mixture into prepared pan; bake in moderate oven about 15 minutes. Turn cake onto baking-paper-covered wire rack. Cover cake with baking paper; cool to room temperature.

4 Grease 22cm springform tin; line side with baking paper, bringing paper 5cm above edge of tin. Cut 22cm-diameter circle from cooled cake; place in prepared tin. Discard remaining cake.

5 Combine cream and extra chocolate in medium saucepan; stir over low heat until smooth. Transfer to large bowl; refrigerate until just cold.

6 Add liqueur to chocolate mixture; beat with electric mixer until mixture changes to a paler colour. Pour mixture into prepared tin; refrigerate about 3 hours or until set.

7 Transfer cake from tin to serving plate; dust with sifted extra cocoa.

tip Do not overbeat the chocolate and liqueur mixture as it will curdle.

mini choc chip almond cakes

preparation time 20 minutes **cooking time** 20 minutes **makes** 18

3 egg whites

90g butter, melted

½ cup (60g) almond meal

¾ cup (120g) icing sugar

¼ cup (35g) plain flour

100g dark eating chocolate, chopped finely

¼ cup (60ml) cream

100g dark eating chocolate, chopped, extra

1 Preheat oven to moderate. Grease 2 x 12-hole mini muffin pans.
2 Place egg whites in medium bowl; whisk lightly with a fork until combined. Add butter, almond meal and sifted icing sugar and flour; using a wooden spoon, stir until just combined. Stir in finely chopped chocolate. Spoon tablespoons of mixture into prepared pan holes. Bake in moderate oven about 15 minutes or until browned lightly and cooked through. Turn onto wire racks to cool.
3 Combine cream and extra chocolate in a medium heatproof bowl over a pan of simmering water; stir until just melted. Stand until thickened. Spoon chocolate mixture over tops of almond cakes.

tips This recipe can be made a day ahead. Almond cakes are suitable to freeze.
Chocolate mixture is suitable to microwave.

rich truffle mud cake

preparation time 15 minutes (plus cooling and refrigeration time) **cooking time** 1 hour **serves** 12 to 14

This very rich cake is perfect for the grand finale to a dinner party, and should be made a day ahead and served cold. The cake is almost like a huge truffle in texture; note that no flour is used.

6 eggs

½ cup (110g) firmly packed brown sugar

400g dark eating chocolate, melted

1 cup (250ml) double cream

⅓ cup (80ml) cointreau

1 Preheat oven to moderate. Grease deep 22cm-round cake pan; line base and side with baking paper.

2 Beat eggs and sugar in large bowl with electric mixer about 5 minutes or until thick and creamy. With motor operating, gradually beat in barely warm chocolate; beat until combined.

3 Using metal spoon, gently fold in combined cream and liqueur. Pour mixture into prepared pan. Place pan in baking dish; pour enough boiling water into dish to come halfway up side of pan.

4 Bake cake in moderate oven 30 minutes. Cover loosely with foil; bake about 30 minutes. Discard foil; cool cake in pan.

5 Turn cake onto serving plate, cover; refrigerate overnight. Serve dusted with a little sifted cocoa powder, if desired.

tips Any liqueur can be substituted for the citrus-flavoured cointreau, if you prefer; try rum or frangelico.
Cake will keep for up to four days in an airtight container in the refrigerator.
This cake is delicious served with raspberries and raspberry coulis.

cakes

black forest cake

preparation time 35 minutes (plus cooling time) **cooking time** 1 hour 50 minutes **serves** 12

250g butter

1 tablespoon instant coffee powder

1½ cups (375ml) hot water

200g dark eating chocolate, chopped

2 cups (440g) caster sugar

1½ cups (225g) self-raising flour

1 cup (150g) plain flour

¼ cup (25g) cocoa powder

2 eggs

2 teaspoons vanilla essence

600ml whipping cream

¼ cup (60ml) kirsch

2 x 425g cans cherries, drained, seeded

1 Preheat oven to slow. Grease deep 23cm-round cake pan, line base and side with baking paper; grease paper well.

2 Melt butter in medium saucepan, stir in combined coffee and hot water, then chocolate and sugar; stir over low heat, without boiling, until smooth. Transfer to large bowl, cool until warm. Beat mixture on low speed with electric mixer; gradually beat in sifted dry ingredients, in three batches. Beat in eggs, one at a time, then essence. Pour into prepared pan. Bake in slow oven about 1¾ hours. Stand in pan 5 minutes before turning onto wire rack to cool.

3 Beat cream until firm peaks form. Trim top of cake to make it flat. Split cake into three layers. Place one layer on serving plate, brush with one-third of the kirsch, top with one-third of the cream and half of the cherries. Repeat layering once more, then top with cake-top. Brush top of cake with remaining kirsch; spread with remaining cream.

tips Cake will keep for up to 3 days, covered, in the refrigerator.
Decorate the cake with fresh cherries and chocolate shavings, if desired.

flourless chocolate hazelnut cake

preparation time 20 minutes (plus cooling time) **cooking time** 1 hour **serves** 8

⅓ cup (35g) cocoa powder

⅓ cup (80ml) hot water

150g dark eating chocolate, melted

150g butter, melted

1⅓ cups (295g) firmly packed brown sugar

1 cup (100g) hazelnut meal

4 eggs, separated

1 tablespoon cocoa powder, extra

1 Preheat oven to moderate. Grease deep 20cm-round cake pan; line base and side with baking paper.

2 Blend cocoa with the water in large bowl until smooth. Stir in chocolate, butter, sugar, meal and egg yolks.

3 Beat egg whites in small bowl with electric mixer until soft peaks form; fold into chocolate mixture in two batches.

4 Pour mixture into prepared pan; bake, uncovered, in moderate oven about 1 hour. Stand cake in pan 15 minutes; turn onto wire rack, top-side up, to cool. Dust with sifted extra cocoa.

tips Our flourless cake confirms that marrying hazelnuts and chocolate in a recipe is a match made in heaven. If you wish, you can roast, skin and process whole hazelnuts to make the meal.
Similarly, you can dot the top of the finished cake with whole roasted nuts before you serve it, either warm or at room temperature.

warm chocolate polenta cakes
with chocolate sauce

preparation time 20 minutes **cooking time** 30 minutes **makes** 8

125g softened butter

⅔ cup (150g) caster sugar

1¼ cups (150g) almond meal

¼ cup (25g) cocoa powder

50g dark eating chocolate, grated

2 eggs

½ cup (85g) instant polenta

⅓ cup (80ml) milk

CHOCOLATE SAUCE

125g dark eating chocolate, chopped

½ cup (125ml) cream

1 Preheat oven to moderately slow. Grease 8 x ⅓-cup (80ml) individual oval pans, line the bases with baking paper.

2 Beat butter and sugar in a small bowl with an electric mixer until light and fluffy. Add almond meal, sifted cocoa and chocolate, mix until just combined. Add eggs one at a time, beating well between additions. Stir in combined polenta and milk.

3 Divide mixture among prepared tins. Bake in moderately slow oven about 30 minutes or until cooked when tested. Turn onto a wire rack to cool slightly. Make chocolate sauce; serve with warm cakes.
CHOCOLATE SAUCE Combine chocolate and cream in a heatproof bowl; stir over a pan of simmering water until melted.

tips This recipe can be made a day ahead. Cakes are suitable to freeze. Sauce is suitable to microwave.
Recipe can be made in round muffin pan.

chocolate mocha dacquoise terrine

preparation time 20 minutes (plus cooling and refrigeration time) **cooking time** 45 minutes **serves** 12

A classic dacquoise is a layered meringue sandwiched with a butter-cream filling. It is served cold, often with a complementary seasonal fruit, or sometimes with nuts mixed into the butter cream.

4 egg whites

1 cup (220g) caster sugar

2 tablespoons cocoa powder

200g dark eating chocolate, chopped coarsely

¾ cup (180ml) cream

2 teaspoons cocoa powder, extra

MOCHA BUTTER CREAM

1 tablespoon instant coffee powder

2 tablespoons boiling water

100g unsalted butter, softened

2¼ cups (360g) icing sugar

1 Preheat oven to slow. Line each of three oven trays with baking paper; draw a 10cm x 25cm rectangle on each baking-paper-lined tray.

2 Beat egg whites in medium bowl with electric mixer until soft peaks form. Gradually add sugar, beating after each addition until sugar dissolves; fold in sifted cocoa.

3 Spread meringue mixture evenly over drawn rectangles; bake, uncovered, in slow oven about 45 minutes or until meringue is dry. Turn off oven; cool meringues in oven with door ajar.

4 Meanwhile, stir chocolate and cream in small saucepan over low heat until smooth, transfer to small bowl; refrigerate until firm. Beat chocolate mixture with electric mixer about 20 seconds or until just changed in colour.

5 Make mocha butter cream.

6 Place one meringue layer on serving plate; spread with half of the chocolate mixture, then top with half of the butter cream. Top with another meringue layer; spread with remaining chocolate mixture, then with remaining butter cream. Top with last meringue layer, cover; refrigerate 3 hours or overnight. To serve, dust with sifted extra cocoa powder.

MOCHA BUTTER CREAM Dissolve coffee powder with the boiling water in small bowl; cool 10 minutes. Beat butter in small bowl with electric mixer until pale in colour; gradually add icing sugar, beating until combined. Beat in coffee mixture.

white chocolate and macadamia muffins

preparation time 10 minutes **cooking time** 20 minutes **makes** 6

2 cups (300g) self-raising flour

⅔ cup (150g) caster sugar

¾ cup (140g) white choc chips

½ cup (75g) toasted macadamias, chopped coarsely

60g butter, melted

¾ cup (180ml) milk

1 egg, beaten lightly

1 Preheat oven to moderately hot. Grease six-hole (¾-cup/180ml) texas muffin pan.

2 Sift flour and sugar into large bowl; stir in remaining ingredients. Divide mixture among holes of prepared pan.

3 Bake muffins in moderately hot oven about 20 minutes. Stand muffins in pan a few minutes before turning onto wire rack.

rich chocolate meringue cake

preparation time 15 minutes **cooking time** 1 hour 30 minutes **serves** 8

8 egg whites

1 cup (220g) caster sugar

60g dark cooking chocolate, chopped finely

¼ cup (60g) finely chopped glacé figs

¼ cup (50g) finely chopped seeded prunes

¾ cup (45g) stale breadcrumbs

¼ cup (25g) cocoa powder

1 tablespoon icing sugar

1 tablespoon cocoa powder, extra

1 Preheat oven to very slow. Grease 22cm springform tin; line base and side with baking paper.

2 Beat egg whites in medium bowl with electric mixer until soft peaks form. Add sugar, 1 tablespoon at a time, beating until sugar dissolves between each addition. Fold in chocolate, fruit, breadcrumbs and sifted cocoa.

3 Spoon mixture into prepared tin; bake in very slow oven 1½ hours. Cool in oven with door ajar.

4 Dust with combined sifted icing sugar and extra cocoa; serve with whipped cream, if desired.

tip Serve with fresh strawberries or cherries, if desired.

cakes

chocolate melting moments

preparation time 15 minutes (plus cooling time) cooking time 10 minutes makes 28

125g butter, chopped

2 tablespoons icing sugar

¾ cup (110g) plain flour

2 tablespoons cornflour

2 tablespoons cocoa powder

¼ cup (85g) chocolate hazelnut spread

1 Preheat oven to moderate. Lightly grease two oven trays.
2 Beat butter and sugar in small bowl with electric mixer until light and fluffy. Stir in sifted dry ingredients, in two batches.
3 Spoon mixture into piping bag fitted with 5mm fluted tube. Pipe directly onto prepared trays, allowing 3cm between each biscuit; bake in moderate oven about 10 minutes or until biscuits are firm. Stand biscuits 5 minutes; transfer to wire rack to cool. Sandwich biscuits with spread to serve.

tip Strawberry or raspberry jam can also be used instead of chocolate hazelnut spread.

triple-choc cookies

preparation time 10 minutes cooking time 10 minutes makes 36

125g butter, chopped

½ teaspoon vanilla extract

1¼ cups (250g) firmly packed brown sugar

1 egg

1 cup (150g) plain flour

¼ cup (35g) self-raising flour

1 teaspoon bicarbonate of soda

⅓ cup (35g) cocoa powder

½ cup (85g) chopped raisins

½ cup (95g) milk choc chips

100g white eating chocolate, chopped coarsely

100g dark eating chocolate, chopped coarsely

1 Preheat oven to moderate. Lightly grease two oven trays.
2 Beat butter, extract, sugar and egg in small bowl with electric mixer until smooth; do not overbeat. Stir in sifted dry ingredients, then raisins, choc chips and white and dark chocolate.
3 Drop level tablespoons of mixture onto prepared trays, allowing 5cm between each cookie; bake in moderate oven about 10 minutes. Stand cookies 5 minutes; transfer to wire rack to cool.

tips For a firmer cookie, bake an extra 2 minutes.
Serve these cookies with hot chocolate for a late-night treat.

biscuits and slices

choc-hazelnut cookie sandwiches

preparation time 25 minutes (plus refrigeration time) **cooking time** 10 minutes **makes** 30

80g butter, chopped

1 teaspoon vanilla extract

¼ cup (55g) caster sugar

1 egg

½ cup (50g) hazelnut meal

¾ cup (110g) plain flour

¼ cup (25g) cocoa powder

1 tablespoon cocoa powder, extra

CHOC-HAZELNUT CREAM

100g dark eating chocolate, melted

50g butter, softened

⅓ cup (110g) chocolate hazelnut spread

1 Beat butter, extract, sugar and egg in small bowl with electric mixer until light and fluffy; stir in hazelnut meal with sifted flour and cocoa. Enclose dough in plastic wrap; refrigerate about 1 hour or until firm.
2 Preheat oven to moderate. Lightly grease two oven trays.
3 Roll dough between two sheets of baking paper until 3mm thick. Using 4cm-fluted cutter, cut 60 rounds from dough. Place rounds on prepared trays; bake in moderate oven about 8 minutes. Stand biscuits 5 minutes; transfer onto wire rack to cool.
4 Make choc-hazelnut cream; spoon into piping bag fitted with large fluted tube. Pipe cream onto one biscuit; sandwich with another biscuit. Place on wire rack set over tray; repeat with remaining biscuits and cream. When all sandwiches are on rack, dust with extra sifted cocoa.
CHOC-HAZELNUT CREAM Beat cooled chocolate, butter and spread in small bowl with electric mixer until thick and glossy.

choc nut biscotti

preparation time 35 minutes (plus cooling time) **cooking time** 50 minutes **makes** 60

1 cup (220g) caster sugar

2 eggs

1⅔ cups (250g) plain flour

1 teaspoon baking powder

1 cup (150g) toasted shelled pistachios

½ cup (70g) slivered almonds

¼ cup (25g) cocoa powder

1 Preheat oven to moderate.
2 Whisk sugar and eggs in medium bowl. Stir in sifted flour, baking powder and nuts; mix to a sticky dough.
3 Knead dough on lightly floured surface until smooth. Divide dough into two portions. Using floured hands, knead one portion on lightly floured surface until smooth, but still slightly sticky; divide into four pieces.
4 Roll each piece into 25cm log shape. Knead remaining portion with cocoa until smooth, divide into two pieces. Roll each piece of chocolate mixture into 25cm log shape.
5 Place one chocolate log on lightly greased oven tray. Place a plain log on each side, press gently together. Repeat with remaining logs.
6 Bake in moderate oven about 30 minutes or until browned lightly. Cool on tray 10 minutes. Reduce oven to slow.
7 Using a serrated knife, cut logs diagonally into 5mm slices. Place slices, in single layer, on ungreased oven trays.
8 Bake in slow oven about 20 minutes or until dry and crisp, turning halfway through cooking; cool on wire racks.

chocolate chip cookies

preparation time 40 minutes (plus refrigeration time) **cooking time** 15 minutes **makes** 40

Originally called toll house cookies, these American biscuits were invented by the owner of the Toll House Inn, Ruth Graves Wakefield, in the 1930s in Massachusetts. Ruth added bits of dark chocolate to her favourite cookie dough, expecting them to melt during baking. Instead, the chocolate held its shape and became delicate and creamy – and the classic chocolate chip cookie was born!

250g butter, softened

1 teaspoon vanilla extract

¾ cup (165g) caster sugar

¾ cup (165g) firmly packed brown sugar

1 egg

2¼ cups (335g) plain flour

1 teaspoon bicarbonate of soda

300g dark cooking chocolate, chopped finely

1 Preheat oven to moderate.
2 Beat butter, extract, sugars and egg in small bowl with electric mixer until light and fluffy. Transfer to large bowl.
3 Stir combined sifted flour and soda, in two batches, into egg mixture. Stir in chocolate, cover; refrigerate 1 hour.
4 Roll level tablespoons of the dough into balls; place on greased oven trays 3cm apart. Bake, uncovered, in moderate oven about 12 minutes. Cool cookies on trays.

fudgy-wudgy chocolate cookies

preparation time 10 minutes **cooking time** 10 minutes **makes** 24

125g butter, chopped

1 teaspoon vanilla extract

1¼ cups (250g) firmly packed brown sugar

1 egg

1 cup (150g) plain flour

¼ cup (35g) self-raising flour

1 teaspoon bicarbonate of soda

⅓ cup (35g) cocoa powder

½ cup (85g) raisins

¾ cup (100g) toasted macadamia nuts, chopped coarsely

½ cup (95g) dark choc chips

100g dark cooking chocolate, chopped coarsely

1 Preheat oven to moderate. Line three oven trays with baking paper.
2 Beat butter, extract, sugar and egg in medium bowl with electric mixer until smooth. Stir in combined sifted flours, soda and cocoa; stir in raisins, nuts, choc chips and dark chocolate.
3 Drop rounded tablespoons of mixture onto prepared trays about 4cm apart; press each with fork to flatten slightly. Bake in moderate oven 10 minutes. Stand 5 minutes; transfer cookies to wire rack to cool.

tips Cookies can be made up to four days ahead; store in an airtight container. Other nuts, such as walnuts or pecans, can be used instead of macadamias.

chocolate florentines

preparation time 25 minutes **cooking time** 35 minutes **makes** 20

30g butter

2 tablespoons brown sugar

1 tablespoon golden syrup

¼ teaspoon ground ginger

2 tablespoons plain flour

1 tablespoon finely chopped glacé apricots

1 tablespoon finely chopped glacé cherries

¼ cup (20g) flaked almonds

75g dark eating chocolate, melted

1 Preheat oven to moderate. Combine butter, sugar and syrup in a pan. Stir over low heat until sugar dissolves. Bring to boil. Using a candy thermometer, bring mixture to 114°C, or, when a small amount is dropped into cold water and can be rolled into a soft ball.

2 Remove from heat, stir in ginger, flour, apricots, cherries and almonds. Drop level teaspoons of mixture on a greased oven tray, leaving 6cm between each. Cook six florentines at a time.

3 Bake about 7 minutes or until browned. Neaten edges while hot; stand florentines for 1 minute; transfer to a wire rack to cool.

4 Spread cooled chocolate thinly over flat side of each florentine; run a fork through chocolate in a wavy pattern. Stand chocolate-side-up until set.

tip Florentines can be made a day ahead. Store in an airtight container in a cool, dry place.

mocha hazelnut biscotti

preparation time 20 minutes (plus cooling time) **cooking time** 50 minutes **makes** 50

1¼ cups (185g) hazelnuts

3 eggs

½ cup (100g) firmly packed brown sugar

½ cup (110g) caster sugar

1½ cups (225g) plain flour

1 cup (150g) self-raising flour

⅓ cup (35g) cocoa powder

2 teaspoons instant coffee powder

2 tablespoons frangelico

100g dark eating chocolate, grated finely

1 Preheat oven to moderate. Spread nuts in single layer on oven tray; bake in moderate oven about 5 minutes or until the skins begin to split. Rub nuts firmly in clean tea towel to remove skins.

2 Beat eggs and sugars in medium bowl with electric mixer until smooth and changed in colour. Stir in sifted flours and cocoa, combined coffee and liqueur, chocolate and nuts; mix to a firm dough.

3 Gently knead dough on floured surface until smooth; divide dough in half. Shape each half into a 7cm x 20cm log. Place logs on greased large oven tray. Bake, uncovered, in moderate oven about 30 minutes or until firm. Cool on tray 15 minutes.

4 Using a serrated knife, cut logs diagonally into 5mm slices; place slices, in single layer, on ungreased oven trays. Bake in moderate oven 15 minutes or until both sides are dry and crisp; cool. Serve with coffee, if desired.

tip This recipe can be made two weeks ahead. Suitable to freeze.

biscuits and slices

55

triple chocolate brownies

preparation time 15 minutes **cooking time** 40 minutes **makes** 18

125g butter, chopped

200g dark eating chocolate, chopped finely

¾ cup (165g) caster sugar

2 eggs, beaten lightly

1 cup (150g) plain flour

150g white eating chocolate, chopped

100g milk eating chocolate, chopped

cocoa powder or icing sugar, for dusting

1 Preheat oven to moderate. Grease deep 19cm-square cake pan, line base and sides with baking paper.

2 Combine butter and dark chocolate in large saucepan; stir over very low heat until melted. Remove from heat.

3 Stir in sugar, then eggs. Stir in sifted flour, then chopped chocolate. Spread mixture into prepared pan.

4 Bake in moderate oven about 35 minutes or until brownie is firm to touch. Cool in pan.

5 Cut into squares. Serve dusted with sifted cocoa or icing sugar, if desired.

tip This recipe can be made 4 days ahead. Suitable to freeze.

chocolate and peanut butter swirl

preparation time 15 minutes (plus standing time) **cooking time** 10 minutes **makes** about 72

360g white eating chocolate, chopped coarsely

½ cup (140g) smooth peanut butter

400g dark chocolate, chopped coarsely

1 Grease 20cm x 30cm slice pan; line base and sides with baking paper, extending 5cm above long edges of pan.

2 Stir white chocolate in small heatproof bowl over simmering water until smooth; cool 5 minutes. Add peanut butter; stir until smooth.

3 Stir dark chocolate in small heatproof bowl over simmering water until smooth; cool slightly.

4 Drop alternate spoonfuls of white chocolate mixture and dark chocolate into prepared pan. Gently shake pan to level mixture; pull a skewer backwards and forwards through mixture several times for a marbled effect. Stand at room temperature about 2 hours or until set; cut into small pieces.

tip Chocolate suitable to melt in microwave oven; heat on medium (55%) about 1 minute, pausing to stir twice.

chocolate macadamia slice

preparation time 15 minutes (plus refrigeration time) **cooking time** 5 minutes **makes** 30

200g butter, chopped

⅓ cup (115g) golden syrup

⅓ cup (35g) drinking chocolate

¼ cup (25g) cocoa powder

500g plain sweet biscuits, chopped finely

½ cup (75g) toasted macadamias, chopped coarsely

200g dark eating chocolate

1 Line 20cm x 30cm slice pan with plastic wrap.
2 Combine butter, syrup, drinking chocolate and sifted cocoa in medium saucepan; stir over medium heat until mixture is smooth. Add biscuits and nuts; stir to combine.
3 Press mixture into prepared pan, cover; refrigerate until firm.
4 Stir chocolate in medium heatproof bowl over simmering water until smooth. Spread chocolate over slice; refrigerate, uncovered, until firm. Cut into pieces to serve.

tip Macadamias can be replaced with any other variety of nut.

chocolate panforte

preparation time 25 minutes (plus standing time) **cooking time** 55 minutes **makes** 30

Rice paper can be found in specialist-food stores and some delicatessens.

2 sheets rice paper

¾ cup (110g) plain flour

2 tablespoons cocoa powder

½ teaspoon ground cinnamon

½ teaspoon ground ginger

½ cup (150g) coarsely chopped glacé figs

½ cup (85g) dried dates, seeded, halved

½ cup (125g) coarsely chopped glacé peaches

¼ cup (50g) red glacé cherries, halved

¼ cup (50g) green glacé cherries, halved

½ cup (80g) toasted blanched almonds

½ cup (75g) toasted unsalted cashews

½ cup (75g) toasted hazelnuts

½ cup (75g) toasted macadamia nuts

⅓ cup (120g) honey

⅓ cup (75g) caster sugar

⅓ cup (75g) firmly packed brown sugar

2 tablespoons water

100g dark eating chocolate, melted

1 Preheat oven to moderately slow. Grease 20cm sandwich pan; line base with rice paper sheets.
2 Sift flour, cocoa and spices into large bowl; stir in fruit and nuts.
3 Combine honey, sugars and the water in small saucepan; stir over heat, without boiling, until sugar dissolves. Simmer; uncovered, without stirring, 5 minutes. Pour hot syrup, then chocolate, into nut mixture; stir until well combined. Press mixture firmly into prepared pan.
4 Bake in moderately slow oven about 45 minutes; cool in pan.
5 Remove panforte from pan; wrap in foil. Stand overnight; cut into thin wedges to serve.

no-bowl choc-chip slice

preparation time 10 minutes (plus cooling time) **cooking time** 30 minutes **makes** about 18

90g butter, melted

1 cup (100g) plain sweet biscuit crumbs

1½ cups (285g) dark choc chips

1 cup (70g) shredded coconut

1 cup (140g) crushed mixed nuts

395g can sweetened condensed milk

1 Preheat oven to moderate. Grease 23cm-square slab pan; line base and sides with baking paper.
2 Pour butter into prepared pan; sprinkle evenly with biscuit crumbs, choc bits, coconut and nuts. Drizzle with condensed milk.
3 Bake in moderate oven about 30 minutes. Cool in pan; cut into pieces.

chocolate cream fudge

preparation time 5 minutes (plus standing time) **cooking time** 20 minutes **makes** 49

It is important to use a candy thermometer in this recipe in order to get the correct consistency when making the fudge.

1½ cups (330g) caster sugar

½ cup (100g) firmly packed brown sugar

60g dark cooking chocolate, chopped coarsely

2 tablespoons glucose syrup

½ cup (125ml) cream

¼ cup (60ml) milk

40g butter

1 Grease deep 15cm-square cake pan.
2 Combine sugars, chocolate, syrup, cream and milk in small saucepan; stir over heat, without boiling, until sugar dissolves. Using pastry brush dipped in hot water, brush down side of pan to dissolve any sugar crystals; bring to a boil. Boil, uncovered, without stirring, about 10 minutes or until syrup reaches 116°C on candy thermometer. Remove pan immediately from heat, leaving candy thermometer in syrup; add butter, do not stir. Cool fudge about 20 minutes or until syrup drops to 40°C on candy thermometer.
3 Stir fudge with wooden spoon about 10 minutes or until a small amount dropped from the spoon holds its shape. Spread fudge into prepared pan; cover with foil. Stand at room temperature about 3 hours or until fudge sets. Turn fudge out of pan; trim edges. Cut into 2cm squares.

no-bake chocolate slice

preparation time 15 minutes (plus refrigeration time) **cooking time** 5 minutes **makes** 24

200g white marshmallows

1 tablespoon water

90g butter, chopped

200g dark eating chocolate, chopped coarsely

125g plain sweet biscuits, chopped coarsely

½ cup (125g) halved glacé cherries

½ cup (75g) toasted hazelnuts

½ cup (50g) walnuts

200g dark eating chocolate, melted, extra

60g butter, melted, extra

1   Grease two 8cm x 25cm bar pans; line bases and sides with baking paper, extending 2cm above long edges of pans.

2   Combine marshmallows, the water and butter in medium saucepan. Stir constantly over low heat until marshmallows are melted. Remove pan from heat. Add chocolate; stir until melted.

3   Add biscuits, cherries and nuts to marshmallow mixture; stir gently until ingredients are combined. Spread mixture evenly into prepared pans (do not crush biscuits). Cover; refrigerate 1 hour.

4   Combine extra chocolate and extra butter; spread mixture evenly over slices. Refrigerate 1 hour or until firm. Remove slices from pans. Peel away paper; cut each into 12 pieces.

tips Slice can be made a week ahead and kept, covered, in refrigerator. Pecans can be used instead of walnuts, if preferred.

hazelnut caramel slice

preparation time 15 minutes (plus refrigeration time) **cooking time** 35 minutes **makes** about 20

200g butter, chopped

½ cup (50g) cocoa powder

2 cups (440g) firmly packed brown sugar

1 teaspoon vanilla extract

2 eggs, beaten lightly

1½ cups (225g) plain flour

200g dark eating chocolate, melted, cooled

1 tablespoon vegetable oil

CARAMEL FILLING

180g butter, chopped

½ cup (110g) caster sugar

2 tablespoons golden syrup

¾ cup (180ml) sweetened condensed milk

1¼ cups (175g) toasted hazelnuts

1   Preheat oven to moderately slow. Grease 20cm x 30cm slice pan; line base and two long sides with baking paper.

2   Combine butter and cocoa in medium saucepan; stir over low heat until smooth. Add sugar; stir until dissolved. Remove from heat; add extract, egg and sifted flour, mix well. Spread mixture into prepared pan, bake in moderately slow oven 20 minutes; cool.

3   Make caramel filling. Quickly spread filling evenly over base; refrigerate at least 30 minutes or until firm. Combine chocolate and oil in small bowl, spread over caramel filling; refrigerate until set. Cut into pieces.
CARAMEL FILLING Combine butter, sugar, syrup and condensed milk in medium saucepan; stir over low heat until butter is melted. Increase heat to medium and simmer, stirring, about 10 minutes or until mixture is dark caramel in colour. Remove from heat; stir in hazelnuts.

tip Slice can be made 2 days ahead and kept, covered, in refrigerator.

chocolate rum and raisin slice

preparation time 10 minutes (plus cooling time) **cooking time** 35 minutes **makes** about 15

125g butter, chopped

200g dark eating chocolate, chopped

½ cup (110g) caster sugar

1 cup (170g) coarsely chopped raisins

2 eggs, beaten lightly

1½ cups (225g) plain flour

1 tablespoon dark rum

1 Preheat oven to moderately slow. Grease 19cm x 29cm slice pan.

2 Combine butter, chocolate, sugar and raisins in medium saucepan; stir over low heat until chocolate is melted. Cool to room temperature. Stir in remaining ingredients, mix well; spread mixture into prepared pan.

3 Bake in moderately slow oven about 30 minutes or until just firm; cool in pan. Serve dusted with sifted icing sugar, if desired.

tip This slice can be made a week ahead; store in an airtight container.

snickers rocky road

preparation time 15 minutes (plus refrigeration time) **cooking time** 5 minutes **makes** 54 squares

We have taken a traditional rocky road recipe and given it a new look by adding snickers bars and toasted, rather than plain, marshmallows.

4 x 60g snickers bars, chopped coarsely

1 cup (35g) rice bubbles

150g toasted marshmallows, chopped coarsely

1 cup (150g) toasted unsalted peanuts

400g milk eating chocolate, chopped coarsely

2 teaspoons vegetable oil

1 Grease 19cm x 29cm slice pan. Line base and two long sides with baking paper, extending paper 2cm above sides of pan.

2 Combine snickers, rice bubbles, marshmallows and nuts in large bowl. Stir chocolate and oil in small saucepan over low heat until smooth. Cool 5 minutes.

3 Pour chocolate mixture into snickers mixture; mix until well combined. Spoon rocky road mixture into prepared pan; refrigerate, covered, about 30 minutes or until set. Remove from pan, trim edges of mixture; cut into 3cm squares. Store, covered, in the refrigerator.

chocolate almond tart

preparation time 35 minutes (plus freezing time) **cooking time** 35 minutes **serves** 4

50g dark eating chocolate, chopped coarsely

¼ cup (55g) caster sugar

1 tablespoon cocoa powder

½ cup (60g) almond meal

20g cold unsalted butter, chopped finely

2 eggs

2 teaspoons brandy

2 sheets ready-rolled puff pastry

1 Process chocolate, sugar, cocoa and almond meal in food processor until chocolate is chopped finely. Add butter and process until mixture begins to come together.

2 Add 1 egg and brandy; process to combine.

3 Cut one pastry sheet into 12cm x 24cm rectangle; cut the other into 14cm x 24cm rectangle. Leaving a 2cm border along all sides, cut even slits in centre of larger pastry sheet at 1.5cm intervals. Place smaller sheet on greased oven tray; spread centre with chocolate mixture, leaving a 2cm border. Brush edges with a little of the remaining beaten egg.

4 Top with other pastry sheet, press edges together. Freeze 10 minutes.

5 Preheat oven to moderately hot.

6 Brush pastry lightly with remaining beaten egg. Bake about 35 minutes or until golden.

tips This tart can be made 8 hours ahead. Suitable to freeze.

pastries and tarts

gourmet chocolate tart

preparation time 40 minutes (plus refrigeration time) **cooking time** 40 minutes **serves** 8

2 eggs

2 egg yolks

¼ cup (55g) caster sugar

250g dark eating chocolate, melted

200g butter, melted

TART SHELL

1½ cups (240g) plain flour

½ cup (110g) caster sugar

140g cold butter, chopped

1 egg, beaten lightly

1 Make tart shell, baking in moderately hot oven as instructed below, then reducing oven temperature to moderate.

2 Whisk eggs, egg yolks and sugar in medium heatproof bowl over simmering water about 15 minutes or until light and fluffy. Gently whisk chocolate and butter into egg mixture.

3 Pour mixture into shell. Bake, uncovered, in moderate oven about 10 minutes or until filling is set; cool 10 minutes. Refrigerate 1 hour. Serve dusted with cocoa powder, if desired.
TART SHELL Blend or process flour, sugar and butter until crumbly; add egg, process until ingredients just come together. Knead dough on floured surface until smooth. Enclose in plastic wrap; refrigerate 30 minutes. Grease 24cm-round loose-base flan tin. Roll dough between sheets of baking paper until large enough to line prepared tin. Lift dough onto tin; press into side, trim edge, prick base all over with fork. Cover; refrigerate 30 minutes. Preheat oven to moderately hot. Place tin on oven tray; cover dough with baking paper, fill with dried beans or rice. Bake, uncovered, in moderately hot oven 10 minutes. Remove paper and beans carefully from tin; bake, uncovered, in moderately hot oven about 5 minutes or until tart shell browns lightly. Cool to room temperature.

chocolate hazelnut croissants

preparation time 15 minutes **cooking time** 15 minutes **makes** 8

2 sheets ready-rolled puff pastry

⅓ cup (110g) chocolate hazelnut spread

30g dark eating chocolate, grated finely

25g butter, melted

1 tablespoon icing sugar

1 Preheat oven to hot. Lightly grease two oven trays.

2 Cut pastry sheets diagonally to make four triangles each. Spread chocolate hazelnut spread over triangles, leaving a 1cm border; sprinkle each evenly with grated chocolate.

3 Roll triangles, starting at wide end; place 3cm apart on prepared trays with the tips tucked under and the ends slightly curved in to form crescent shape. Brush croissants with melted butter.

4 Bake, uncovered, in hot oven about 12 minutes or until croissants are browned lightly and cooked through. Dust croissants with icing sugar; serve warm or at room temperature.

rich chocolate coconut tart

preparation time 10 minutes (plus refrigeration time) **cooking time** 40 minutes **serves** 12

1 cup (90g) desiccated coconut

1 egg white, beaten lightly

¼ cup (55g) caster sugar

300ml cream

300g dark eating chocolate, chopped finely

4 egg yolks

2 teaspoons coffee-flavoured liqueur

1 Preheat oven to slow. Grease 20cm non-stick springform pan.
2 Combine coconut, egg white and caster sugar. Press mixture evenly over base and 4cm up side of prepared pan. Bake, uncovered, about 40 minutes or until golden. Cool.
3 Heat cream until almost boiling. Add chocolate, stir until smooth; cool slightly.
4 Whisk egg yolks and liqueur into chocolate; strain. Pour chocolate mixture into coconut shell. Refrigerate 6 hours or until set.
5 Cut into thin wedges to serve.

tips To make it easier to remove pan base from tart, place base in upside down before lining with biscuit.
This tart can be made up to 8 hours ahead.
The tart filling is suitable to microwave.

chocolate butterscotch tartlets

preparation time 5 minutes (plus refrigeration time) **cooking time** 10 minutes **makes** 12

12 frozen tartlet cases

¼ cup (55g) firmly packed brown sugar

20g butter

¼ cup (60ml) cream

150g dark eating chocolate, chopped coarsely

¼ cup (60ml) cream, extra

2 tablespoons coarsely chopped toasted hazelnuts

1 tablespoon cocoa powder

1 Bake tartlet cases according to manufacturer's instructions.

2 Meanwhile, heat combined sugar, butter and cream in small saucepan, stirring until sugar dissolves. Reduce heat; simmer, uncovered, without stirring, 2 minutes. Cool 5 minutes. Stir in chocolate and extra cream; refrigerate 10 minutes.

3 Divide mixture among tartlet cases, sprinkle with nuts and sifted cocoa.

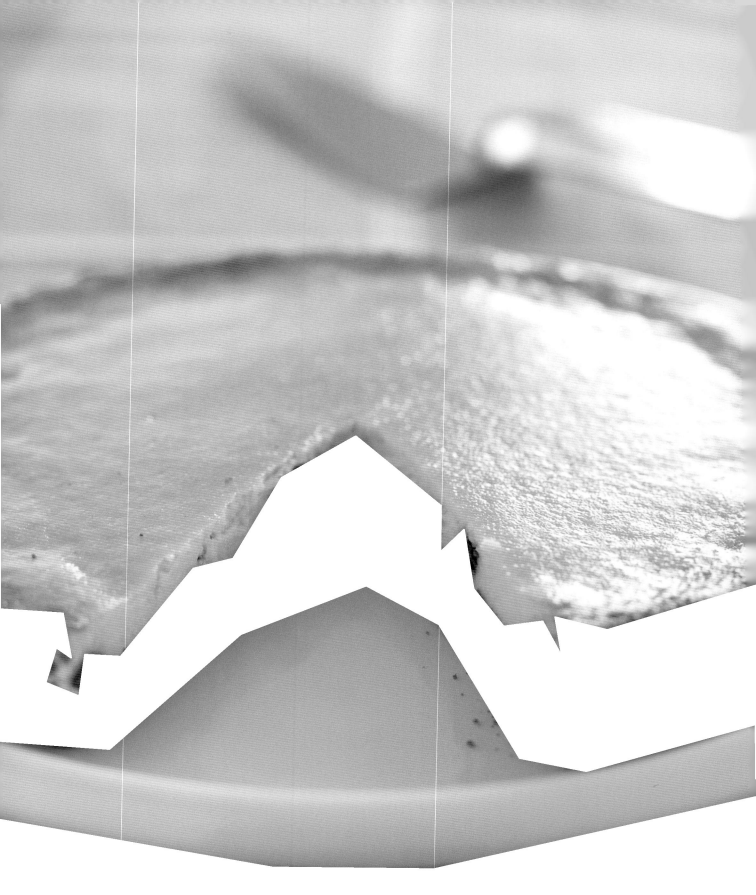

low-fat chocolate ricotta tart

preparation time 15 minutes (plus refrigeration time) **cooking time** 35 minutes **serves** 8

¼ cup (35g) white self-raising flour

¼ cup (40g) wholemeal self-raising flour

2 tablespoons caster sugar

2 teaspoons cocoa powder

30g low-fat margarine

2 teaspoons water

1 egg yolk

RICOTTA FILLING

150g low-fat ricotta

1 egg

1 egg yolk

¼ cup (70g) low-fat plain yogurt

¼ cup (55g) caster sugar

2 teaspoons white plain flour

2 tablespoons dark choc chips

2 teaspoons coffee-flavoured liqueur

1 Grease 18cm-round loose-based flan tin.
2 Process flours, sugar, sifted cocoa and spread until crumbly; add the water and egg yolk, process until ingredients just cling together. Knead dough gently on lightly floured surface until smooth, cover; refrigerate 30 minutes.
3 Preheat oven to moderately hot.
4 Press dough into prepared tin; cover with baking paper large enough to extend 5cm over edge, fill with dried beans or rice. Bake, on oven tray, in moderately hot oven 10 minutes; remove beans and paper. Bake further 5 minutes or until pastry is lightly browned; cool.
5 Reduce oven to moderate. Make ricotta filling.
6 Pour ricotta filling into cooled tart case; bake, uncovered, in moderate oven about 20 minutes. Cool; refrigerate until firm.
   RICOTTA FILLING Using electric mixer, beat ricotta, egg, egg yolk, yogurt, sugar and flour in medium bowl until smooth. Stir in choc bits and liqueur.

waffles with ice-cream and chocolate peanut sauce

preparation time 5 minutes **cooking time** 5 minutes **serves** 4

½ cup (125ml) cream

2 x 60g snickers bars, chopped coarsely

200g waffles

vanilla ice-cream for serving

1　Heat cream gently in a small saucepan, add snickers bars and stir until melted and combined.

2　Toast waffles until crisp.

3　Divide waffles among serving plates or bowls, top with scoops of ice-cream and drizzle with sauce.

tips The sauce can be made several hours ahead; reheat gently. Sauce is suitable to microwave.

caramel chocolate tarts

preparation time 25 minutes (plus standing time) **cooking time** 15 minutes **makes** 24

1 cup (150g) plain flour

90g butter, chopped

¼ cup (55g) caster sugar

400g can sweetened condensed milk

30g butter, extra

2 tablespoons golden syrup

100g dark eating chocolate, melted

1 Preheat oven to moderate. Grease two 12-hole 1½-tablespoon (30ml) mini-muffin pans.

2 Blend or process flour, butter and sugar until ingredients just come together. Press level tablespoons of butter mixture into each hole of prepared pans to form tart cases. Bake in moderate oven about 10 minutes or until browned lightly.

3 Meanwhile, combine condensed milk, extra butter and syrup in small saucepan; stir until smooth. Do not boil.

4 Pour hot caramel filling into hot cases; return to oven about 3 minutes or until caramel begins to brown around the edges. Stand 2 minutes; using a pointed vegetable knife, gently remove tarts from pans. Cool.

5 Spread top of cooled tarts with melted chocolate; stand until set.

tip The tarts can be made up to 3 days ahead. Refrigerate, covered, in an airtight container.

choc-brownies with caramel sauce

preparation time 10 minutes **cooking time** 25 minutes **serves** 6

80g butter, chopped

150g dark cooking chocolate, chopped coarsely

¾ cup (150g) firmly packed brown sugar

2 eggs, beaten lightly

1 teaspoon vanilla essence

¾ cup (110g) plain flour

300ml vanilla ice-cream

⅓ cup (45g) candied (vienna) almonds, chopped coarsely

CARAMEL SAUCE

⅔ cup (160ml) cream

60g butter, chopped

¾ cup (150g) firmly packed brown sugar

1 Preheat oven to hot. Grease 6-hole (¾ cup/180ml) texas muffin pan.
2 Combine butter, chocolate and sugar in medium saucepan; stir over medium heat until smooth.
3 Stir in egg, essence and flour; divide mixture among muffin pan holes. Cover pan tightly with foil; bake in hot oven about 20 minutes. Remove foil; stand 5 minutes.
4 Make caramel sauce.
5 Place brownies on serving plates; top with ice-cream, caramel sauce and candied almonds.
   CARAMEL SAUCE Combine ingredients in small saucepan; stir over medium heat until smooth. Simmer 2 minutes.

tip The caramel sauce and chocolate-melting stage for the brownies can be done in a microwave oven.

desserts

white chocolate fondue

preparation time 10 minutes **cooking time** 5 minutes **serves** 4

180g white eating chocolate, chopped coarsely

½ cup (125ml) cream

1 tablespoon malibu

1 cup (130g) strawberries

1 large banana (230g), chopped coarsely

150g fresh pineapple, chopped coarsely

8 slices (35g) almond bread

16 marshmallows (100g)

1 Combine chocolate and cream in small saucepan, stir over low heat until smooth; stir in liqueur. Transfer fondue to serving bowl.

2 Place fondue in centre of dining table; serve remaining ingredients on a platter with skewers.

tip Fondue can be served with any of your favourite fruits.

desserts

85

chocolate, pear and hazelnut self-saucing pudding

preparation time 30 minutes **cooking time** 1 hour 10 minutes **serves** 6

100g dark eating chocolate, chopped coarsely

50g butter, chopped

⅔ cup (160ml) milk

¼ cup (25g) hazelnut meal

⅔ cup (100g) toasted hazelnuts, chopped coarsely

1 cup (220g) firmly packed brown sugar

1 cup (150g) self-raising flour

1 egg, beaten lightly

2 medium pears (460g)

300ml cream

2 tablespoons icing sugar

2 tablespoons frangelico

FUDGE SAUCE

1¾ cups (430ml) water

100g butter, chopped

1 cup (220g) firmly packed brown sugar

½ cup (50g) cocoa powder, sifted

1 Preheat oven to moderate. Grease shallow 3-litre (12-cup) baking dish.

2 Stir chocolate, butter and milk in small saucepan over low heat until smooth. Transfer to large bowl; stir in hazelnut meal, nuts and brown sugar, then flour and egg.

3 Peel and core pears; slice thinly. Place pear slices, slightly overlapping, in prepared dish; top with chocolate mixture.

4 Make fudge sauce; pour over chocolate mixture. Bake, uncovered, in moderate oven about 1 hour. Stand 10 minutes.

5 Meanwhile, beat cream, icing sugar and liqueur in small bowl with electric mixer until soft peaks form. Serve pudding with frangelico cream.
   FUDGE SAUCE Stir ingredients in small saucepan over low heat until smooth.

tip The frangelico can be omitted from the whipped cream mixture for an alcohol-free dessert.

chocolate soufflé with raspberry coulis

preparation time 15 minutes **cooking time** 20 minutes **serves** 4

Today, a coulis is generally regarded to be a thick puree or sauce usually made from fruit such as tomatoes or berries; however, the original French culinary use of the word referred to the juices that flow into the pan from meat as it cooks.

1 tablespoon caster sugar

50g butter

1 tablespoon plain flour

200g dark eating chocolate, melted

2 egg yolks

4 egg whites

¼ cup (55g) caster sugar, extra

RASPBERRY COULIS

150g frozen raspberries, thawed

2 tablespoons caster sugar

4 cloves

½ cup (125ml) dry red wine

1 Preheat oven to moderately hot. Grease four ¾-cup (180ml) soufflé dishes. Sprinkle insides of dishes evenly with sugar; shake away any excess. Place dishes on oven tray.

2 Melt butter in small saucepan, add flour; cook, stirring, about 2 minutes or until mixture thickens and bubbles. Remove from heat; stir in chocolate and egg yolks. Transfer to large bowl.

3 Beat egg whites in small bowl with electric mixer until soft peaks form. Gradually add extra sugar, one tablespoon at a time, beating until sugar dissolves between additions. Fold egg white mixture into chocolate mixture, in two batches.

4 Divide soufflé mixture among prepared dishes; bake, uncovered, in moderately hot oven about 15 minutes or until soufflés are puffed.

5 Meanwhile, make raspberry coulis.

6 Serve soufflés with raspberry coulis.
   RASPBERRY COULIS Combine raspberries and sugar in small saucepan; cook, without boiling, until sugar dissolves. Add cloves and wine; bring to a boil. Reduce heat; simmer, uncovered, about 5 minutes or until coulis thickens. Strain coulis into medium jug.

chocolate berry meringues

preparation time 20 minutes (plus cooling time) **cooking time** 45 minutes **serves** 4

If raspberries are not in season, you can vary the proportions of strawberries and blueberries to make a total of 550g.

3 egg whites

¾ cup (165g) caster sugar

1 tablespoon cocoa powder

300ml whipping cream

150g raspberries

250g strawberries, quartered

150g blueberries

1 Preheat oven to very slow. Grease and line oven tray with baking paper. Draw four 13cm-diameter circles on paper.

2 Beat egg whites in small bowl with electric mixer until soft peaks form. Add sugar, 1 tablespoon at a time, beating until sugar dissolves between each addition; fold in sifted cocoa.

3 Spread meringue mixture over drawn circles. Bake in very slow oven about 45 minutes or until firm; cool meringues in oven with door ajar.

4 Beat cream in small bowl with electric mixer until lightly whipped; top meringues with cream and berries.

tip When separating eggs, take care to avoid any yolk getting into the whites or they will not beat to the correct meringue consistency.

cookies and cream cheesecake

preparation time 20 minutes (plus refrigeration time) **cooking time** 5 minutes **serves** 12

THE first recorded mention of cheesecake dates all the way back to ancient Greece but it gained wide popularity in the Jewish delis of New York. Our version takes its flavour from the much-loved cookies and cream ice-cream variety.

250g plain chocolate biscuits

150g butter, melted

2 teaspoons gelatine

¼ cup (60ml) water

1½ cups (360g) packaged cream cheese, softened

300ml cream

1 teaspoon vanilla extract

½ cup (110g) caster sugar

180g white eating chocolate, melted

150g cream-filled chocolate biscuits, quartered

50g dark eating chocolate, melted

1 Line base of 23cm springform tin with baking paper.
2 Blend or process plain chocolate biscuits until mixture resembles fine breadcrumbs. Add butter; process until just combined. Using hand, press biscuit mixture evenly over base and 3cm up side of prepared tin, cover; refrigerate 20 minutes.
3 Sprinkle gelatine over the water in small heatproof jug; stand jug in small saucepan of simmering water. Stir until gelatine dissolves; cool 5 minutes.
4 Beat cheese, cream, extract and sugar in medium bowl with electric mixer until smooth. Stir in gelatine mixture and white chocolate; fold in quartered biscuits. Pour cheesecake mixture over biscuit mixture in tin, cover; refrigerate about 3 hours or until set. Drizzle with dark chocolate to serve.

tip Place dark chocolate in a small plastic bag with the corner snipped off to help you drizzle it evenly over the cheesecake.

chocolate hazelnut self-saucing puddings

preparation time 15 minutes **cooking time** 25 minutes **serves** 4

½ cup (125ml) milk

40g dark chocolate, chopped coarsely

50g butter

⅓ cup (35g) cocoa powder

½ cup (75g) self-raising flour

¼ cup (25g) hazelnut meal

⅓ cup (75g) caster sugar

⅔ cup (150g) firmly packed brown sugar

1 egg, beaten lightly

¾ cup (180ml) water

40g butter, chopped, extra

200g vanilla ice-cream

CHOCOLATE HAZELNUT SAUCE

½ cup (125ml) cream

2 tablespoons brown sugar

50g dark chocolate, chopped finely

⅓ cup (110g) chocolate hazelnut spread

1 tablespoon frangelico

1 Preheat oven to moderate. Grease four 1-cup (250ml) ovenproof dishes.
2 Stir milk, chocolate, butter and half of the cocoa in small saucepan over low heat until smooth.
3 Combine flour, hazelnut meal, caster sugar and half of the brown sugar in medium bowl. Add chocolate mixture and egg; stir until combined. Divide mixture among prepared dishes.
4 Stir the water, extra butter, remaining brown sugar and remaining cocoa in small saucepan over low heat until smooth. Pour hot mixture gently and evenly over puddings; bake puddings, uncovered, in moderate oven about 25 minutes. Stand 5 minutes.
5 Meanwhile, make chocolate hazelnut sauce.
6 Serve puddings topped with ice-cream and chocolate hazelnut sauce.
   CHOCOLATE HAZELNUT SAUCE Combine cream and sugar in small saucepan. Bring to a boil; remove from heat. Add chocolate; stir until smooth. Add spread and liqueur; stir until smooth.

tip This dessert is best served hot because the sauce is quickly absorbed by the puddings.

chocolate nut bavarois with raspberry sauce

preparation time 30 minutes (plus refrigeration time) **cooking time** 5 minutes **serves** 6

1 cup (250ml) milk

½ cup (165g) chocolate hazelnut spread

4 egg yolks

¼ cup (55g) caster sugar

2 teaspoons gelatine

1 tablespoon water

300ml cream

RASPBERRY SAUCE

200g raspberries

2 tablespoons icing sugar

1 Combine milk and spread in small saucepan. Stir over heat until spread melts; bring to a boil. Transfer to medium bowl.

2 Beat egg yolks and caster sugar in small bowl with electric mixer until thick and creamy; gradually stir into chocolate mixture.

3 Sprinkle gelatine over the water in small heatproof jug; stand in small saucepan of simmering water, stirring, until gelatine dissolves. Stir gelatine mixture into warm chocolate mixture; cool to room temperature.

4 Beat cream in small bowl with electric mixer until soft peaks form; fold into chocolate mixture. Divide bavarois mixture among six ¾-cup (180ml) serving glasses; refrigerate about 4 hours.

5 Make raspberry sauce. Serve bavarois topped with raspberry sauce.
RASPBERRY SAUCE Push raspberries through sieve into small bowl; discard seeds. Stir in icing sugar.

tips If fresh raspberries are not available, use frozen raspberries, thawed. As a guide, when dissolved gelatine is added to a mixture, both should be roughly the same temperature.

desserts

chocolate marquise

preparation time 30 minutes (plus refrigeration and freezing time) **cooking time** 15 minutes **serves** 10

A marquise is based on the classic French bavarois (bavarian cream), a cold dessert composed of a rich egg custard, whipped cream and any of a number of flavourings, the choice being up to the cook – chocolate being our favourite.
The chocolate sponge roll in this recipe is made with plain as opposed to self-raising flour because the beaten eggs are enough to aerate the mixture.

¾ cup (180ml) cream

100g dark eating chocolate, chopped coarsely

4 egg yolks

2 eggs

½ cup (110g) caster sugar

300ml cream, extra

¼ cup (60ml) orange-flavoured liqueur

¾ cup (75g) coarsely grated dark eating chocolate

2 teaspoons finely grated orange rind

CHOCOLATE SPONGE

4 eggs

⅔ cup (150g) caster sugar

⅓ cup (50g) plain flour

1 tablespoon cocoa powder

1 Make chocolate sponge.

2 Line base and long sides of 14cm x 21cm loaf pan with baking paper. Cut two rectangles from cooled sponge, one measuring 13cm x 21cm, the other 11cm x 19cm; discard remaining sponge.

3 Combine cream and chopped chocolate in small saucepan; stir over low heat until smooth. Beat egg yolks, eggs and sugar in medium bowl with electric mixer until thick and creamy; with motor operating, gradually beat hot chocolate mixture into egg mixture. Cover; refrigerate about 30 minutes or until mixture thickens slightly.

4 Meanwhile, beat extra cream in small bowl with electric mixer until soft peaks form; fold cream, liqueur, grated chocolate and rind into cooled chocolate mixture.

5 Place smaller rectangle of sponge in prepared pan; pour over chocolate mixture, top with remaining sponge rectangle. Cover with foil; freeze until firm. Turn marquise out onto board; stand at room temperature about 5 minutes or until softened slightly. Slice thickly, serve with fresh berries macerated in the same orange-flavoured liqueur, if desired.

CHOCOLATE SPONGE Preheat oven to moderate. Grease 25cm x 30cm swiss roll pan; line base with baking paper. Beat eggs and sugar in small bowl with electric mixer until thick and creamy; transfer to large bowl. Fold in triple-sifted combined flour and cocoa; spread mixture into prepared pan. Bake, uncovered, in moderate oven about 10 minutes. Cool 10 minutes.

soft-centred chocolate cakes with warm sour cherry sauce

preparation time 20 minutes **cooking time** 15 minutes **serves** 6

Sour cherry jam is made from morello cherries, which have a dark mahogany-red skin and flesh. The combination of cherries and chocolate make an irresistible dessert.

185g dark chocolate, chopped coarsely

185g butter, chopped

3 egg yolks

⅓ cup (50g) plain flour

4 eggs

⅓ cup (75g) caster sugar

350g jar sour cherry jam

1   Preheat oven to moderate. Grease six-hole ¾-cup (180ml) texas muffin pan. Sprinkle with a little plain flour; tilt to coat holes, shake off any excess.

2   Place chocolate and butter in small saucepan; stir over low heat until mixture is smooth. Transfer to large bowl; stir in yolks and flour.

3   Beat eggs and sugar in small bowl with electric mixer about 5 minutes or until light and fluffy. Fold egg mixture into chocolate mixture; spoon mixture into prepared pan. Bake in moderate oven about 10 minutes; cakes should be soft in the centre. Stand 5 minutes; remove carefully from pan.

4   Meanwhile, melt jam in small saucepan over low heat; blend or process until smooth, strain. Return jam to saucepan, add a little water to give pouring consistency; bring to a boil. Skim surface; stand 5 minutes.

5   Serve warm soft-centred chocolate cakes drizzled with warm sauce.

tip Sour cherry jam can be found in most supermarkets.

white chocolate, irish cream and berry trifle

preparation time 25 minutes (plus cooling and refrigeration time) **serves** 10

5 eggs

¾ cup (165g) caster sugar

500g mascarpone

300ml cream

⅓ cup (25g) ground espresso coffee

2 cups (500ml) boiling water

1 cup (250ml) irish cream liqueur

2 x 250g packets savoiardi sponge finger biscuits

75g white eating chocolate, grated

500g strawberries, hulled

300g raspberries

75g white eating chocolate, extra

1   Beat eggs and sugar in a medium bowl with an electric mixer about 10 minutes or until thick and creamy.

2   Beat mascarpone and cream in a large bowl with an electric mixer until thick. Fold egg mixture into mascarpone mixture.

3   Place coffee and boiling water in a coffee plunger; stand 2 minutes before plunging. Strain coffee through a fine sieve into a medium heatproof bowl; stir in liqueur.

4   Dip half of the biscuits, one at a time, briefly in coffee mixture until just starting to soften. Line the base of two shallow 2-litre (8 cup) or one 3.5-litre (14 cup) capacity serving dish with biscuits.

5   Spread half of the mascarpone mixture over the biscuits. Top with grated chocolate. Slice half of the strawberries and place over chocolate. Repeat layering process with remaining biscuits, coffee mixture and mascarpone mixture. Cover; refrigerate several hours or overnight.

6   Slice remaining strawberries; place on top of trifle with raspberries. Using a vegetable peeler, make chocolate curls from extra white chocolate. Sprinkle curls over berries just before serving.

tip This trifle is best made a day ahead.

chocolate bread and butter pudding

preparation time 20 minutes **cooking time** 50 minutes **serves** 6

Rich egg-and-butter brioche can be made in the shape of a loaf or roll, but the most recognisable variation is perhaps the 'brioche à tête' ('a roll with a head') that is formed by placing a small ball of dough on top of a larger one. One of France's first regional specialities, the brioche of Normandy dates back to the early 1400s.

1½ cups (375ml) milk

2 cups (500ml) cream

⅓ cup (75g) caster sugar

1 vanilla bean

4 eggs

2 small brioche (200g), sliced thickly

100g dark eating chocolate, chopped coarsely

⅓ cup (40g) coarsely chopped toasted pecans

1 Preheat oven to moderate.

2 Combine milk, cream and sugar in small saucepan. Split vanilla bean in half lengthways; scrape seeds into pan, then place pod in pan. Stir over heat until hot; strain into large heatproof jug, discard pod.

3 Whisk eggs in large bowl; whisking constantly, add hot milk mixture.

4 Grease shallow 2-litre (8 cup) ovenproof dish; layer brioche, chocolate and nuts, overlapping brioche slightly, in dish. Pour hot milk mixture over top.

5 Place dish in large baking dish; add enough boiling water to come halfway up sides of dish. Bake, uncovered, in moderate oven about 45 minutes or until pudding sets. Remove pudding from baking dish; stand 5 minutes before serving.

desserts

white chocolate and strawberry cheesecake

preparation time 25 minutes (plus refrigeration time) **cooking time** 5 minutes **serves** 10

185g digestive biscuits

80g butter, melted

3 teaspoons gelatine

2 tablespoons water

500g packets cream cheese, softened

400g can sweetened condensed milk

300ml cream

150g white eating chocolate, melted

500g large strawberries, hulled, halved

¼ cup (80g) strawberry jam, warmed, strained

1 tablespoon lemon juice

1　Grease 23cm springform tin.

2　Blend or process biscuits until mixture resembles fine breadcrumbs. Add butter; process until combined. Using hand, press biscuit mixture evenly over base of prepared tin, cover; refrigerate about 30 minutes or until firm.

3　Sprinkle gelatine over the water in small heatproof jug; stand jug in small saucepan of simmering water. Stir until gelatine dissolves. Cool 5 minutes.

4　Meanwhile, beat cheese and condensed milk in medium bowl with electric mixer until smooth. Beat cream in small bowl with electric mixer until soft peaks form.

5　Stir warm gelatine mixture into cheese mixture; fold in cream and chocolate. Pour cheesecake mixture into prepared tin, spreading evenly over biscuit base. Cover; refrigerate overnight.

6　Arrange strawberries on top of cheesecake; brush strawberries with combined jam and juice.

desserts

silky chocolate mousse

preparation time 15 minutes (plus cooling and refrigeration time) **cooking time** 5 minutes **serves** 8

300g dark eating chocolate, chopped coarsely

50g butter

3 eggs, separated

1 tablespoon irish cream liqueur

¼ cup (55g) caster sugar

300ml cream, whipped

1 Combine chocolate and butter in small saucepan; stir over low heat until smooth. Remove from heat.

2 Stir in egg yolks, one at a time, then liqueur; transfer mixture to large bowl. Cool to room temperature.

3 Beat egg whites in small bowl with electric mixer until soft peaks form. Gradually add sugar, 1 tablespoon at a time, beating until sugar dissolves between each addition.

4 Meanwhile, fold cream into chocolate mixture, then fold in egg white mixture, in two batches. Divide chocolate mousse among eight ½-cup (125ml) serving dishes. Cover; refrigerate 2 hours or until set.

tips This mousse is best made a day ahead.
The chocolate and butter mixture is suitable to microwave.

desserts

gourmet rocky road

preparation time 20 minutes (plus refrigeration time) **makes** 40 slices

300g toasted marshmallows, chopped coarsely

400g turkish delight, chopped coarsely

¼ cup (40g) toasted blanched almonds, chopped coarsely

½ cup (75g) toasted shelled pistachios

450g white eating chocolate, melted

1 Grease two 8cm x 26cm bar cake pans; line base and sides with baking paper, extending paper 5cm above long sides.

2 Combine marshmallows, turkish delight and nuts in large bowl. Working quickly, stir in chocolate; spread mixture into prepared pans, push mixture down firmly to flatten the top. Refrigerate until set, then cut as desired.

after-dinner treats

white choc, lemon, lime and coconut balls

preparation time 40 minutes (plus refrigeration time) **cooking time** 5 minutes **makes** 30

½ cup (125ml) coconut cream

2 teaspoons finely grated lime rind

2 teaspoons finely grated lemon rind

360g white eating chocolate, chopped coarsely

1¼ cups (85g) shredded coconut

1 Combine coconut cream, rinds and chocolate in small saucepan; stir over low heat until smooth. Transfer mixture to small bowl, cover; refrigerate 3 hours or overnight.

2 Working with a quarter of the chocolate mixture at a time (keeping remainder refrigerated), roll rounded teaspoons into balls; place on tray. Refrigerate truffles until firm.

3 Working quickly, roll truffles in coconut, place in mini patty pans on tray; refrigerate until firm.

mint slice bites

preparation time 20 minutes **cooking time** 30 minutes **makes** 36

125g butter, chopped

200g dark eating chocolate, chopped coarsely

½ cup (110g) caster sugar

2 eggs, beaten lightly

1¼ cups (185g) plain flour

1½ cups (240g) icing sugar

1 teaspoon butter, extra

¼ teaspoon peppermint essence

2 tablespoons milk, approximately

50g dark chocolate, melted, extra

1 Preheat oven to moderate. Grease deep 19cm-square cake pan; line base with baking paper.

2 Combine butter and chocolate in medium saucepan; stir over low heat until chocolate melts. Stir in caster sugar and egg, then flour. Spread mixture into prepared pan; bake in moderate oven about 20 minutes. Stand cake in pan 15 minutes; turn onto wire rack to cool.

3 Meanwhile, combine icing sugar, extra butter and essence in small heatproof bowl; gradually stir in enough milk to make mixture form a thick paste. Stir mixture over small saucepan of simmering water until icing is of spreadable consistency. Spread icing over cake; set at room temperature.

4 Using serrated knife, trim crisp edges from cake. Cut cake into 3cm squares; drizzle each square with extra chocolate.

after-dinner treats

113

dark chocolate and ginger truffles

preparation time 40 minutes (plus refrigeration time) **cooking time** 5 minutes **makes** 30

⅓ cup (80ml) cream

200g dark eating chocolate, chopped coarsely

½ cup (115g) glacé ginger, chopped finely

¼ cup (25g) cocoa powder

1 Combine cream and chocolate in small saucepan; stir over low heat until smooth, stir in ginger. Transfer to small bowl, cover; refrigerate 3 hours or overnight.

2 Working with a quarter of the chocolate mixture at a time (keeping remainder refrigerated), roll rounded teaspoons into balls; place on tray. Refrigerate truffles until firm.

3 Working quickly, roll balls in cocoa, place in mini patty pans on tray; refrigerate truffles until firm.

ALMONDS flat, pointed-ended nuts with pitted brown shell enclosing a creamy white kernel covered by a brown skin.
blanched brown skins removed.
candied (vienna) are toffee-coated almonds.
flaked paper-thin slices.
meal also known as ground almonds; nuts are powdered to a coarse flour texture, for use in baking or as a thickening agent.
slivered small pieces cut lengthways.

BAKE BLIND a cooking term describing a pie shell or pastry case baked before filling is added. To bake blind, ease pastry into required pan or dish, place on oven tray; cover pastry with baking paper, fill with dried rice or proper baking 'beans' (also called pie weights). Bake in moderately hot oven 10 minutes, remove paper and beans; bake further 10 minutes or until browned lightly. Cool before adding filling.

BAKING PAPER also known as parchment, silicon paper or non-stick baking paper; not to be confused with greaseproof or waxed paper. Used to line pans before cooking, baking and also to make piping bags.

BICARBONATE OF SODA also known as baking soda.

BISCUITS also known as cookies.
butternut snap biscuits containing rolled oats, coconut and golden syrup that resemble anzac biscuits.
savoiardi also known as savoy biscuits, lady's fingers or sponge fingers, these Italian-style crisp fingers are made from sponge cake mixture.

sweet any plain sweet biscuit (cookie) can be used; chocolate biscuits used were uniced.

BRANDY spirit distilled from wine.

BREADCRUMBS, STALE one- or two-day-old bread made into crumbs by grating, blending or processing.

BRIOCHE rich French yeast-risen bread made with butter and eggs. Available from pâtisseries or specialty bread shops.

BUTTER use salted or unsalted (sweet) butter; 125g is equal to 1 stick butter.

CASHEWS we used unsalted roasted cashews in this book. They are available from health food stores and most supermarkets.

CHERRIES soft stone fruit varying in colour from yellow to dark red. Sweet cherries are eaten whole and in desserts while sour cherries such as the bitter morello variety are used in jams, preserves, pies and savoury dishes, particularly as an accompaniment to game birds and meats.
glacé are cooked in heavy sugar syrup and then dried.

CHOCOLATE
choc chips also known as chocolate bits and chocolate morsels; available in milk, white and dark chocolate. Made of cocoa liquor, cocoa butter, sugar and an emulsifier, these hold their shape in baking and are ideal for decorating.
cocoa powder also known as cocoa; dried, unsweetened, roasted and then ground cocoa beans.
dark eating made of cocoa liquor, cocoa butter and sugar.
dark cooking we used premium quality dark cooking chocolate rather than compound.
drinking sweetened cocoa powder.
hazelnut spread also known as Nutella; is a commercial spread.
milk primarily for eating.
white we used cooking-quality chocolate.

COCONUT
desiccated unsweetened, concentrated, dried finely shredded coconut.
flaked dried flaked coconut flesh.
milk not the juice found inside the fruit, which is known as coconut water, but the diluted liquid from the second pressing from the white meat of a mature coconut (the first pressing produces coconut cream). Available in cans and cartons at supermarkets.
shredded thin strips of dried coconut.

CREAM CHEESE fresh cheese with a soft, spreadable texture and mild flavour.

CORNFLOUR also known as cornstarch; used as a thickening agent in cooking.

DATES, DRIED sweeter and richer than fresh dates, eaten as a snack or used in sweet dishes.

ESSENCES also known as extracts; generally the by-product of distillation of plants. Can be set in alcohol or in a more pure form in glycerine.

FLOUR
plain an all-purpose flour, made from wheat.
self-raising plain flour sifted with baking powder in the proportion of 1 cup flour to 2 teaspoons baking powder.
soya flour made from ground soya beans.
wholemeal plain also known as all-purpose wholewheat flour, has no baking powder added.

GANACHE rich mixture of chocolate, butter and cream used as a filling for cakes or confectionery and to decorate desserts.

GELATINE we used powdered gelatine; also available in sheet form known as leaf gelatine.

GLACÉ FIGS figs preserved in a sugar syrup.

GLACÉ GINGER fresh ginger root preserved in sugar syrup. Crystallised ginger can be substituted if rinsed with warm water and dried before using.

GLUCOSE SYRUP also known as liquid glucose, made from wheat starch; used in jam and confectionery and available at health food stores and supermarkets.

GOLDEN SYRUP a by-product of refined sugarcane; pure maple syrup or honey can be substituted.

GROUND GINGER also known as powdered ginger; used as a flavouring in cakes, pies and puddings but cannot be substituted for fresh ginger.

HAZELNUTS also known as filberts; plump, grape-size, rich, sweet nut having a brown inedible skin that is removed by rubbing heated nuts together vigorously in a tea towel.

JAM also known as preserve or conserve; most often made from fruit.

glossary

LAMINGTON PAN 20cm x 30cm slab cake pan, 3cm deep.

LIQUEURS

cointreau citrus-flavoured liqueur.

frangelico hazelnut-flavoured liqueur.

irish cream we used baileys, a smooth and creamy natural blend of fresh irish cream, the finest irish spirits, irish whisky, cocoa and vanilla.

kahlua coffee-flavoured liqueur.

kirsch cherry-flavoured liqueur.

malibu coconut-flavoured rum.

tia maria coffee-flavoured liqueur.

LOW-FAT YOGURT we used yogurt with a fat content of less than 0.2%.

MACADAMIA native to Australia, rich and buttery nut; store in refrigerator because of high oil content.

MASCARPONE a fresh, unripened, smooth, triple cream cheese with a rich, sweet taste, slightly acidic.

MARSHMALLOWS pink and white; made from sugar, glucose, gelatine and cornflour.

MILK we used full-cream homogenised milk unless otherwise specified.

buttermilk sold alongside fresh milk products in supermarkets and is commercially made, by a method similar to yogurt. Despite the implication of its name, it is low in fat and is a good substitute for dairy products such as cream or sour cream, good in baking and in salad dressings.

evaporated unsweetened canned milk from which water has been extracted by evaporation.

sweetened condensed a canned milk product consisting of milk with more than half the water content

removed and sugar added to the remaining milk.

PEANUT BUTTER peanuts ground to a paste; available in crunchy and smooth varieties.

PEANUTS not in fact a nut but the pod of a legume.

PECAN NUTS native to the united states and now grown locally; golden-brown, buttery and rich. Good in savoury as well as sweet dishes; especially good in salads.

PISTACHIO NUTS pale green, delicately flavoured nut inside hard off-white shells. To peel, soak shelled nuts in boiling water for about 5 minutes; drain, then pat dry with absorbent paper. Rub skins with cloth to peel.

POLENTA also known as cornmeal; a flour-like cereal made of dried corn (maize) sold ground in several different textures; also the name of the dish made from it.

PRUNES commercially or sun-dried plums.

RAISINS dried sweet grapes.

READY-ROLLED PUFF PASTRY packaged sheets of frozen puff pastry, available from supermarkets.

RICE BUBBLES puffed rice product made with malt extract which contains gluten.

RICE PAPER there are two products sold as rice paper.

banh trang made from rice paste and stamped into rounds; store well at room temperature. They're quite brittle and will break if dropped; dipped momentarily in water they become pliable wrappers for fried food and uncooked vegetables. Make good spring-roll wrappers.

glossy rice paper an edible, translucent paper made from a

dough of water combined with the pith of an Asian shrub called the rice-paper plant (or rice-paper tree). The fine, glossy paper is edible and is very useful in the making of biscuits, such as macaroons. In China and Japan, where the tree is widely cultivated, rice paper is used to make artificial flowers. This variety, generally imported from Holland, is whiter than the other and looks more like a grainy sheet of paper. It is used in confectionery making and baking, and not eaten uncooked.

RICOTTA soft white cow milk cheese; roughly translates as 'cooked again'. It's made from whey, a by-product of other cheese making, to which fresh milk and acid are added. Ricotta is a sweet, moist cheese with a fat content of around 8.5% and a slightly grainy texture.

RUM, DARK we prefer to use an underproof rum (not overproof) for a more subtle flavour.

SNICKERS BARS made from chocolate, peanuts, glucose, sugar, milk powder, butter and egg white.

SUGAR we used coarse, granulated table sugar, also known as crystal sugar, unless otherwise specified.

brown an extremely soft, fine granulated sugar retaining molasses for its characteristic colour and flavour.

caster also known as superfine or finely granulated table sugar.

icing mixture also known as confectioners' sugar or powdered sugar; pulverised granulated sugar crushed together with a small amount of (about 3%) cornflour added.

SWISS ROLL PAN (also known as a jelly-roll pan) measures 26cm x 32cm in area; its slightly raised sides (averaging 2cm in

height) help contain the mixture (usually cake batters, egg mixtures or various light doughs) being baked in it, preventing the swiss roll, sponge, roulade, jam roll, slice, pizza base, etc. from rising. Often the baked item is removed from the pan and rolled while still hot and malleable, then later unrolled, spread with various sweet or savoury fillings, and rolled again before slicing. Can also be a rectangular baking pan having 2cm-deep sides used to make a swiss roll, genoise, jam roll, roulade, jelly roll or even pizza base; usually 26cm x 32cm in area.

TURKISH DELIGHT jellied sweet usually containing almonds or pistachio nuts. Often coloured pink or green, cut into cubes and coated in icing sugar.

VANILLA

bean dried, long, thin pod from a tropical golden orchid grown in central and South America and Tahiti; the minuscule black seeds inside the bean are used to impart a luscious vanilla flavour in baking and desserts. A whole bean can be placed in the sugar container to make the vanilla sugar often called for in recipes.

essence obtained from vanilla beans infused in alcohol and water.

extract obtained from vanilla beans infused in water. A non-alcoholic version of essence.

ice-cream we used a good quality ice-cream having 5g of fat per 100ml.

WALNUTS cream-coloured, wrinkled nuts with brown skin, formed into two distinct halves.

WHITE VINEGAR made from spirit of cane sugar.

glossary

A

after-dinner treats
    dark chocolate and
        ginger truffles 114
    gourmet rocky road 110
    mint slice bites 113
    white choc, lemon, lime
        and coconut balls 113
almond and dark chocolate
    torte 23
almond cakes, mini choc
    chip 32
almond chocolate tart 66

B

bavarois, chocolate nut,
    with raspberry sauce 97
berry chocolate meringues
    90
berry, irish cream, and white
    chocolate trifle 102
biscuits, see also slices
    choc-hazelnut cookie
        sandwiches 51
    choc nut biscotti 51
    chocolate and peanut
        butter swirl 56
    chocolate chip cookies
        52
    chocolate florentines 55
    chocolate melting
        moments 48
    fudgy-wudgy chocolate
        cookies 52
    mocha hazelnut biscotti
        55
    triple-choc cookies 48
    triple chocolate brownies
        56
black forest cake 36
bread and butter pudding,
    chocolate 105
brownies, choc, with
    caramel sauce 82
brownies, triple chocolate
    56
buttermilk cake, chocolate
    11

butterscotch chocolate
    tartlets 74

C

cakes 78, see also tortes
    black forest 36
    chocolate buttermilk 11
    chocolate mocha
        dacquoise terrine 43
    chocolate roulade with
        coffee cream 16
    double-decker mud 27
    family chocolate 7
    flourless chocolate
        hazelnut 39
    gluten-free chocolate 28
    irish cream and dark
        chocolate mousse 31
    low-fat chocolate fudge
        20
    mini choc chip almond
        cakes 32
    mississippi mud 15
    mocha syrup 8
    rich chocolate meringue
        47
    rich truffle mud 35
    soft-centred chocolate
        cakes with warm sour
        cherry sauce 101
    sticky chocolate date 11
    upside-down chocolate
        caramel nut 19
    warm chocolate polenta
        cakes with chocolate
        sauce 40
    white chocolate and
        macadamia muffins
        44
    white chocolate mud 4
caramel chocolate nut cake,
    upside-down 19
caramel chocolate tarts 81
caramel hazelnut slice 63
caramel sauce, choc-
    brownies with 82
caramel topping 19
cheesecake, cookies and
    cream 93

cheesecake, strawberry and
    white chocolate 106
chocolate, see dark
    chocolate; white
    chocolate (note that all
    recipes contain chocolate
    or cocoa)
chocolate filling 11
chocolate icing 24
chocolate sauce 40
chocolate sponge 98
coconut balls, white choc,
    lemon, lime and 113
coconut chocolate tart, rich
    73
coffee, see also mocha
coffee cream, chocolate
    roulade with 16
coffee syrup 8
cookie sandwiches, choc-
    hazelnut 51
cookies, see biscuits
cookies and cream
    cheesecake 93
coulis, raspberry 89
croissants, chocolate
    hazelnut 70

D

dacquoise terrine, chocolate
    mocha 43
dark chocolate
    and almond torte 23
    and ginger truffles 114
    and irish cream mousse
        cake 31
date cake, sticky chocolate
    11
desserts, see also puddings
    choc-brownies with
        caramel sauce 82
    chocolate berry
        meringues 89
    chocolate marquise 98
    chocolate nut bavarois
        with raspberry sauce
        97
    chocolate soufflé with
        raspberry coulis 89

(desserts continued)
    cookies and cream
        cheesecake 93
    silky chocolate mousse
        109
    soft-centred chocolate
        cakes with warm sour
        cherry sauce 101
    white chocolate and
        strawberry cheesecake
        106
    white chocolate fondue
        85
    white chocolate, irish
        cream, and berry trifle
        102
double-decker mud cake
    27

F

family chocolate cake 7
filling, chocolate 11
florentines, chocolate 55
flourless chocolate hazelnut
    cake 39
fondue, white chocolate 85
fudge cake, low-fat
    chocolate 20
fudge, chocolate cream 60
fudge frosting 7
fudge sauce 86
fudgy-wudgy chocolate
    cookies 52

G

ganache, dark chocolate 23
ganache, white chocolate 4
ginger truffles, dark
    chocolate and 114
gluten-free chocolate cake
    28
gourmet chocolate tart 69
gourmet rocky road 110

H

hazelnut caramel slice 63
hazelnut-choc cookie
    sandwiches 51

index **117**

hazelnut chocolate cake,
    flourless 39
hazelnut chocolate
    croissants 70
hazelnut chocolate self-
    saucing puddings 94
hazelnut mocha biscotti 55
hazelnut, pear and
    chocolate self-saucing
    pudding 86

I

icing, chocolate 24
irish cream and dark
    chocolate mousse cake
    31
irish cream, white
    chocolate, and berry trifle
    102

L

lemon, lime, white choc and
    coconut balls 113
low-fat chocolate fudge
    cake 20
low-fat chocolate ricotta
    tart 77

M

macadamia and white
    chocolate muffins 44
macadamia chocolate slice
    59
marquise, chocolate 98
melting moments,
    chocolate 48
meringue
    chocolate berry
        meringues 90
    chocolate mocha
        dacquoise terrine 43
    rich chocolate meringue
        cake 47
mini choc chip almond
    cakes 32
mint slice bites 113
mississippi mud cake 15
mocha, see also coffee
mocha butter cream 43
mocha chocolate dacquoise
    terrine 43
mocha hazelnut biscotti
    55
mocha syrup cake 8
mousse cake, irish cream
    and dark chocolate 31

mousse, silky chocolate 109
mud cake
    double-decker 27
    mississippi 15
    rich truffle 35
    white chocolate 4
muffins, white chocolate
    and macadamia 44

N

no-bake chocolate slice 63
no-bowl choc-chip slice 60
nuts, see also almond;
    hazelnut; macadamia;
    peanut
    nut choc biscotti 51
    nut chocolate bavarois
        with raspberry sauce
        97
    upside-down chocolate
        caramel nut cake 19

P

panforte, chocolate 59
pastries, see also tarts
    chocolate hazelnut
        croissants 70
    waffles with ice-cream
        and chocolate peanut
        sauce 78
peanut butter and
    chocolate swirl 56
peanut chocolate sauce,
    waffles with ice-cream
    and 78
pear, chocolate and
    hazelnut self-saucing
    pudding 86
polenta cakes, warm
    chocolate, with chocolate
    sauce 40
puddings, see also desserts
    chocolate bread and
        butter pudding 105
    chocolate hazelnut
        self-saucing puddings
        94
    chocolate, pear and
        hazelnut self-saucing
        pudding 86

R

raisin and rum slice,
    chocolate 64
raspberry coulis, chocolate
    soufflé with 89

raspberry sauce, chocolate
    nut bavarois with 97
rich chocolate coconut tart
    73
rich chocolate meringue
    cake 47
rich truffle mud cake 35
ricotta tart, low-fat
    chocolate 77
rocky road, gourmet 110
rocky road, snickers 64
roulade, chocolate, with
    coffee cream 16
rum and raisin slice,
    chocolate 64

S

sacher torte 24
sauce, chocolate 40
self-saucing puddings,
    chocolate hazelnut 94
self-saucing puddings,
    chocolate, pear and
    hazelnut 86
silky chocolate mousse 109
slices
    chocolate cream fudge
        60
    chocolate macadamia
        59
    chocolate panforte 59
    chocolate rum and raisin
        64
    hazelnut caramel 63
    no-bake chocolate 63
    no-bowl choc-chip 60
    snickers rocky road 64
snickers bars
    snickers rocky road 64
    waffles with ice-cream
        and chocolate peanut
        sauce 78
soft-centred chocolate
    cakes with warm sour
    cherry sauce 101
soufflé, chocolate, with
    raspberry coulis 89
sour cherry sauce, warm,
    soft-centred chocolate
    cakes with 101
sponge, chocolate 98
sticky chocolate date cake
    11
strawberry and white
    chocolate cheesecake
    106
Swiss roll, see roulade

T

tarts, see also pastries
    caramel chocolate 81
    chocolate almond 66
    chocolate butterscotch
        tartlets 74
    gourmet chocolate 69
    low-fat chocolate ricotta
        77
    rich chocolate coconut
        73
    tart shell 69
terrine, chocolate mocha
    dacquoise 43
toll house cookies, see
    chocolate chip cookies
tortes
    dark chocolate and
        almond 23
    sacher 24
trifle, white chocolate, irish
    cream, and berry 102
triple-choc cookies 48
triple chocolate brownies
    56
truffle mud cake, rich 35
truffles, dark chocolate and
    ginger 114

U

upside-down chocolate
    caramel nut cake 19

W

waffles with ice-cream and
    chocolate peanut sauce
    78
warm chocolate polenta
    cakes with chocolate
    sauce 40
white chocolate
    and macadamia muffins
        44
    and strawberry
        cheesecake 106
    fondue 85
    irish cream, and berry
        trifle 102
    mud cake 4
    white choc, lemon, lime
        and coconut balls 113

conversion chart

Wherever you live, you'll be able to use our recipes with the help of these easy-to-follow conversions. While these conversions are approximate only, the difference between an exact and the approximate conversion of various liquid and dry measures is minimal and will not affect your cooking results.

LIQUID MEASURES

METRIC	IMPERIAL
30ml	1 fluid oz
60ml	2 fluid oz
100ml	3 fluid oz
125ml	4 fluid oz
150ml	5 fluid oz (¼ pint/1 gill)
190ml	6 fluid oz
250ml	8 fluid oz
300ml	10 fluid oz (½ pint)
500ml	16 fluid oz
600ml	20 fluid oz (1 pint)
1000ml (1 litre)	1¾ pints

MEASURING EQUIPMENT

The difference between one country's measuring cups and another's is, at most, within a 2 or 3 teaspoon variance. (For the record, one Australian metric measuring cup holds approximately 250ml.) The most accurate way of measuring dry ingredients is to weigh them. When measuring liquids, use a clear glass or plastic jug with the metric markings. (One Australian metric tablespoon holds 20ml; one Australian metric teaspoon holds 5ml.)

HOW TO MEASURE

When using graduated metric measuring cups, shake dry ingredients loosely into the appropriate cup. Do not tap the cup on a bench or tightly pack the ingredients unless directed to do so. Level top of measuring cups and measuring spoons with a knife. When measuring liquids, place a clear glass or plastic jug with metric markings on a flat surface to check accuracy at eye level.

Note: North America, NZ and the UK use 15ml tablespoons. All cup and spoon measurements are level.

We use large eggs having an average weight of 60g.

DRY MEASURES

METRIC	IMPERIAL
15g	½oz
30g	1oz
60g	2oz
90g	3oz
125g	4oz (¼lb)
155g	5oz
185g	6oz
220g	7oz
250g	8oz (½lb)
280g	9oz
315g	10oz
345g	11oz
375g	12oz (¾lb)
410g	13oz
440g	14oz
470g	15oz
500g	16oz (1lb)
750g	24oz (1½lb)
1kg	32oz (2lb)

LENGTH MEASURES

METRIC	IMPERIAL
3mm	⅛in
6mm	¼in
1cm	½in
2cm	¾in
2.5cm	1in
5cm	2in
6cm	2½in
8cm	3in
10cm	4in
13cm	5in
15cm	6in
18cm	7in
20cm	8in
23cm	9in
25cm	10in
28cm	11in
30cm	12in (1ft)

OVEN TEMPERATURES

These oven temperatures are only a guide. Always check the manufacturer's manual.

	°C (CELSIUS)	°F (FAHRENHEIT)	GAS MARK
Very slow	120	250	½
Slow	150	275-300	1-2
Moderately slow	170	325	3
Moderate	180	350-375	4-5
Moderately hot	200	400	6
Hot	220	425-450	7-8
Very hot	240	475	9

ARE YOU MISSING SOME OF THE WORLD'S FAVOURITE COOKBOOKS?

The Australian Women's Weekly Cookbooks are available from bookshops, cookshops, supermarkets and other stores all over the world. You can also buy direct from the publisher, using the order form below.

TITLE	RRP	QTY	TITLE	RRP	QTY
Almost Vegetarian	£5.99		Great Lamb Cookbook	£5.99	
Asian Meals in Minutes	£5.99		Greek Cooking Class	£5.99	
Babies & Toddlers Good Food	£5.99		Healthy Heart Cookbook	£5.99	
Barbecue Meals In Minutes	£5.99		Indian Cooking Class	£5.99	
Basic Cooking Class	£5.99		Japanese Cooking Class	£5.99	
Beginners Cooking Class	£5.99		Kids' Birthday Cakes	£5.99	
Beginners Simple Meals	£5.99		Kids Cooking	£5.99	
Beginners Thai	£5.99		Lean Food	£5.99	
Best Ever Slimmers' Recipes	£5.99		Low-carb, Low-fat	£5.99	
Best Food	£5.99		Low-fat Feasts	£5.99	
Best Food Desserts	£5.99		Low-fat Food For Life	£5.99	
Best Food Fast	£5.99		Low-fat Meals in Minutes	£5.99	
Best Food Mains	£5.99		Main Course Salads	£5.99	
Cakes Cooking Class	£5.99		Middle Eastern Cooking Class	£5.99	
Caribbean Cooking	£5.99		Midweek Meals in Minutes	£5.99	
Casseroles	£5.99		Muffins, Scones & Breads	£5.99	
Chicken Meals in Minutes	£5.99		New Casseroles	£5.99	
Chinese Cooking Class	£5.99		New Classics	£5.99	
Christmas Cooking	£5.99		New Finger Food	£5.99	
Cocktails	£5.99		Party Food and Drink	£5.99	
Cooking for Friends	£5.99		Pasta Meals in Minutes	£5.99	
Creative Cooking on a Budget	£5.99		Potatoes	£5.99	
Detox	£5.99		Quick Meals in Minutes	£5.99	
Dinner Beef	£5.99		Salads: Simple, Fast & Fresh	£5.99	
Dinner Lamb	£5.99		Saucery	£5.99	
Dinner Seafood	£5.99		Sensational Stir-Fries	£5.99	
Easy Australian Style	£5.99		Short-order Cook	£5.99	
Easy Curry	£5.99		Slim	£5.99	
Easy Spanish-Style	£5.99		Sweet Old Fashioned Favourites	£5.99	
Essential Soup	£5.99		Thai Cooking Class	£5.99	
Freezer, Meals from the	£5.99		Vegetarian Meals in Minutes	£5.99	
French Cooking Class	£5.99		Vegie Food	£5.99	
French Food, New	£5.99		Weekend Cook	£5.99	
Fresh Food for Babies & Toddlers	£5.99		Wicked Sweet Indulgences	£5.99	
Get Real, Make a Meal	£5.99		Wok Meals in Minutes	£5.99	
Good Food Fast	£5.99		TOTAL COST:	£	

NAME

ADDRESS

POSTCODE

DAYTIME PHONE

I ENCLOSE MY CHEQUE/MONEY ORDER FOR £

OR PLEASE CHARGE MY VISA, ACCESS OR MASTERCARD NUMBER

CARD HOLDER'S NAME

EXPIRY DATE

CARDHOLDER'S SIGNATURE

To order: Mail or fax – photocopy or complete the order form above, and send your credit card details or cheque payable to: Australian Consolidated Press (UK), Moulton Park Business Centre, Red House Road, Moulton Park, Northampton NN3 6AQ, phone (+44) (0) 1604 497531, fax (+44) (0) 1604 497533, e-mail books@acpmedia.co.uk Or order online at www.acpuk.com
Non-UK residents: We accept the credit cards listed on the coupon, or cheques, drafts or International Money Orders payable in sterling and drawn on a UK bank. Credit card charges are at the exchange rate current at the time of payment.
Postage and packing UK: Add £1.00 per order plus 50p per book.
Postage and packing overseas: Add £2.00 per order plus £1.00 per book.
Offer ends 30.06.2006

Test Kitchen
Food director *Pamela Clark*
Food editor *Cathie Lonnie*
Assistant food editor *Rochelle Fernandez*

Photographers *Alan Benson, Steve Brown, Ben Dearnley, Louise Lister, Andre Martin, Con Poulos, Brett Stevens, Ian Wallace*

Stylists *Wendy Berecry, Julz Beresford, Janelle Bloom, Kate Brown, Kirsty Cassidy, Marie-Helene Clauzon, Carolyn Fienberg, Jane Hann, Amber Keller, Opel Khan, Sarah O'Brien, Louise Pickford, Suzie Smith*

ACP Books
Editorial director *Susan Tomnay*
Creative director *Hieu Chi Nguyen*
Project editor *Stephanie Kistner*
Editor *Anna Scobie*
Designer *Corey Butler*
Sales director *Brian Cearnes*
Marketing director *Matt Dominello*
Brand manager *Renée Crea*
Production manager *Cedric Taylor*

Chief executive officer *John Alexander*
Group publisher *Pat Ingram*
Publisher *Sue Wannan*
Editorial director (AWW) *Deborah Thomas*

Produced by ACP Books, Sydney.
Printed by Dai Nippon, c/o Samhwa Printing C Ltd, 237-10 Kuro-Dong, Kuro-Ku, Seoul, Korea.
Published by ACP Magazines Ltd,
54 Park St, Sydney;
GPO Box 4088, Sydney, NSW 2001.
Ph: (02) 9282 8618 Fax: (02) 9267 9438.
acpbooks@acpmagazines.com.au
www.acpbooks.com.au
To order books, phone 136 116.
Send recipe enquiries to:
recipeenquiries@acpmagazines.com.au
RIGHTS ENQUIRIES
Laura Bamford, Director ACP Books.
lbamford@acpmedia.co.uk
AUSTRALIA: Distributed by Network Services,
GPO Box 4088, Sydney, NSW 2001.
Ph: (02) 9282 8777 Fax: (02) 9264 3278
networkweb@networkservicescompany.com.au
UNITED KINGDOM: Distributed by Australian
Consolidated Press (UK), Moulton Park
Business Centre, Red House Rd,
Moulton Park, Northampton, NN3 6AQ.
Ph: (01604) 497531 Fax: (01604) 497533
books@acpmedia.co.uk
CANADA: Distributed by Whitecap Books Ltd,
351 Lynn Ave, North Vancouver, BC, V7J 2C4.
Ph: (604) 980 9852 Fax: (604) 980 8197
customerservice@whitecap.ca
www.whitecap.ca
NEW ZEALAND: Distributed by Netlink
Distribution Company, ACP Media Centre,
Cnr Fanshawe and Beaumont Streets,
Westhaven, Auckland.
PO Box 47906, Ponsonby, Auckland, NZ.
Ph: (09) 366 9966 Fax: 0800 277 412
ask@ndc.co.nz
SOUTH AFRICA: Distributed by PSD
Promotions, 30 Diesel Road Isando,
Gauteng Johannesburg.
PO Box 1175, Isando 1600,
Gauteng Johannesburg.
Ph: (2711) 392 6065/6/7
Fax: (2711) 392 6079/80
orders@psdprom.co.za

Clark, Pamela.
The Australian women's weekly chocolate

Includes index.
ISBN 1 86396 534 3.
1. Cookery (Chocolate).
I. Title. II Title: Australian Women's Weekly.

641.6374
© ACP Magazines Ltd 2006
ABN 18 053 273 546